LIKE A RAGING FIRE

A Biography of Maurice N. Eisendrath

Avi M. Schulman

Foreword by Albert Vorspan

UAHC Press
New York

Cover: Silent prayer vigil at Arlington National Cemetery in protest of the Vietnam War, c.1968. From left to right: the Rev. Roger Alling, Jr., Episcopal Diocese, Newark, NJ; the Rev. Martin Luther King, Jr.; the Rev. Ralph Abernathy; Rabbi Maurice N. Eisendrath, president, UAHC; and Rabbi Abraham J. Heschel, Jewish Theological Seminary. (Photo by John C. Goodwin)

Photos appear between pages 62 and 63.

Library of Congress Cataloging-in-Publication Data

Schulman, Avi M.
Like a Raging Fire: A Biography of Maurice N. Eisendrath/Avi M. Schulman; foreword by Albert Vorspan.
p. cm.
Includes bibliographical references.
ISBN 0-8074-0525-6
1. Eisendrath, Maurice Nathan, 1902-1973. 2. Rabbis—United States—Biography. 3. Jewish leadership—United States. 4. Union of American Hebrew Congregations. 5. Reform Judaism—United States—History—20th century. I. Title.
BM755.E45S34   1993
296.8'346'092—dc20
[B]   93-33072
                                                                        CIP

To my parents, Arnold and Birdie Schulman
for their devotion and support.
To Eve,
for her love and understanding.

To our children,
Naomi, Carmiel, and Rebecca
and the future they represent.

ACKNOWLEDGMENTS

This biography began as a rabbinic thesis written under the supervision of Dr. Michael Meyer. I am greatly indebted to him for his encouragement and patience, as well as his concern that my work be precise, logical, and well written.

In the initial stage of my research, Rabbi Edward Paul Cohn graciously informed me of the location of resources about Eisendrath. Rabbi Rachel Hertzman, then serving as an intern at the Religious Action Center (RAC) in Washington, D.C., tirelessly sought out and discovered the RAC's Eisendrath materials. Rabbi David Saperstein, then co-director of the RAC, arranged to ship to the American Jewish Archives these print resources. The staffs of the American Jewish Archives and the Klau Library were helpful in aiding my research. I especially wish to express my appreciation to Mrs. Fannie Zelcer for her marvelous sense of humor and for her assistance in tracking down Eisendrath arcana.

Hebrew Union College-Jewish Institute of Religion Vice President Samuel Greengus, then serving as dean, and HUC-JIR Dean (retired) Lowell McCoy provided me with financial assistance to conduct research in New York. I am grateful to all who agreed to be interviewed by an eager student armed with a tape recorder, notepad, and dozens of questions. The extensive and insightful comments of those interviewed aided me in establishing a balanced view of Maurice Eisendrath. My understanding of the significance of Eisendrath's remarks about Jesus at the 1963 UAHC biennial was enhanced by Dr. Jonathan Sarna's comments on Chapter 6.

I wish to thank Al Vorspan for serving as patron for the publication of this book. No one has better fulfilled Eisendrath's commitment to social action. This book recounts the struggles and accomplishments in which Vorspan played so large a part. My thanks also to Aron Hirt-Manheimer, the skillful editor of this manuscript.

My thanks to three rabbinic colleagues and friends: Rabbi Walli Kaelter for being my lifelong rabbi; Rabbi P. Irving Bloom for his never-failing kindness; and Rabbi Raymond Zwerin for his insights into the world of publishing

Finally, there is one person who has seen every stage of this biography's odyssey: conceptualization, research, writing, editing, and now, publication. I give thanks to my wife, Rabbi Eve Ben-Ora, for sharing this odyssey with me.

CONTENTS

Foreword

Introduction   3

1. "Eisey": 1902 –1926   7

2. Pulpit and Politics: 1926 –1943   15

3. At the Union's Helm: 1943 –1951   26

4. Revival and Expansion: 1951–1963   38

5. "With Moral Indignation and Righteous Protest"   50

6. "Jesus—Man of My People"   63

7. Slowed Steps: 1963 –1973   70

8. Epilogue   77

Footnotes   82

Bibliography   86

Appendix "The State of Our Union," 1959   90

I said, "I will not mention God,
No more will I speak in God's name"—
But [God's word] was like a raging fire in my heart
Shut up in my bones;
I am weary of containing myself,
And I cannot.

Jeremiah 20:9

FOREWORD

This volume fills a large void. How sad that a new generation of Jews has arisen that knew not Joseph—in this case, Maurice N. Eisendrath, who was a major player in the shaping of post–World War II Reform Judaism. As Rabbi Schulman vividly demonstrates in these pages, Eisendrath was a stormy petrel, eager for controversy, a maverick who nonetheless led a major establishment organization. Eisendrath was not content with soaring rhetoric, although he was regarded as a peerless master of the old-school, florid style of oratory. Under his leadership, the Union of American Hebrew Congregations developed NFTY, the National Federation of Temple Youth (now the North American Federation of Temple Youth), and its camp programs, pioneered in Jewish education, organized a regional network to serve the congregations, and moved the UAHC from Cincinnati to New York City.

Eisendrath risked much for the moral imperatives of justice. When congregants in the South threatened to withhold funds in protest against the UAHC stand on civil rights, Eisendrath refused to compromise on what he regarded as a fundamental principle. Similarly, when large and powerful congregations actually left the UAHC in rebellion to condemn the UAHC position against the Vietnam War, Eisendrath was determined to maintain lines of communication and to respect diversity of opinion within the movement, but he would not budge on the right—and duty—of Reform Judaism to speak out on issues of war and peace. He was the founder of the national Commission on Social Action of Reform Judaism, and it was he who inspired the late Kivie Kaplan to make possible the establishment of the Religious Action Center in Washington, D.C. These are living legacies to Eisendrath's yearning for social justice and of Reform Judaism's particular commitment to prophetic Judaism. Reform Judaism has no monopoly on social justice; all branches of Judaism embrace these ethical values. Indeed, Abraham Joshua Heschel, a Conservative rabbi and scholar, was Eisendrath's associate, and inspiration, in many of these causes. But, thanks in part to the historic leadership that Eisendrath embodied, only

Reform as a movement has been serious about social justice—serious in its budget, in its priorities, and in the risks it has been willing to run in the pursuit of that justice.

Picture Eisendrath as a leading religious figure in the civil rights march to Selma. He joined with Martin Luther King, Jr., not only in his struggle for equal rights but also in his campaign against poverty and especially in his opposition to the Vietnam War. Together they led interreligious marches in Washington, using the recently created Religious Action Center as a base for Jewish demonstrations against the war. Indeed, the center was used as an infirmary to care for demonstrators overwhelmed by tear gas.

Eisendrath viewed Christianity with ambivalence. On the one hand, he believed that the poison of anti-Semitism derived principally from church teachings; that the Holocaust would not have been possible without centuries of Christian contempt for and degradation of Jews and Judaism. But for those very reasons, he was deeply moved by the positive changes that transformed Catholicism after World War II. Additionally, he was a strong supporter of interfaith coalitions for social justice. He stood shoulder to shoulder with Christian leaders such as Dana Greeley, a Unitarian minister; Bishop John Wright, the late bishop of Pittsburgh and of the Roman Catholic hierarchy; and Homer Jack, all churchmen who specialized in issues of international peace and the aims of the United Nations.

Eisendrath had his faults, but he was an inspiring leader. For him, prophetic Judaism was not just a nice slogan for sermonizing purposes. It was the core of his faith, the essence of his life. If he took himself seriously it was because he took Judaism so seriously. He truly believed that liberal Judaism had both the mandate and the power to transform the world. After a meeting at which Eisendrath had eloquently described the urgent moral challenges of race and class that must be dealt with by an activist Jewish conscience, a leading Orthodox scholar, who no doubt had a hard time accepting Eisendrath as a rabbi, confided to a colleague, "The man is a better Jew than any of us."

Eisendrath was an assertive and decisive figure, a dramatic

leader who knew where he was going, but he did not surround himself with sycophants and yes people. I recall with nostalgia how Maurice would summon several members of the staff to his office to challenge him and one another on major events of the day—McCarthy; Selma, Alabama; Vietnam; the Six Day War; Watergate—and how they affect UAHC policy and program. He wanted candor, he could handle disagreement and criticism, and he treated us as colleagues and friends, not as spear carriers and underlings.

In the last years of his life, although fighting illness, Eisendrath became increasingly urgent about preserving world peace in the nuclear age. Perhaps quixotically, he saw the forces of religion as the surest foundation for peace and the best corrective to the human tendencies to violence and nationalistic fratricide. Thus, he became a founder of the World Conference on Religion and Peace and, with his wife Rita, traveled the world in behalf of peace. Was he overly romantic about the latent power of religion to help achieve peace? At a press conference inaugurating the World Conference on Religion and Peace, Eisendrath delivered a peroration on the power of faith to eliminate war. A cynical reporter asked, "Isn't getting Judaism, Christianity, and Islam together more likely to touch off World War III than anything else?" For Eisendrath, the justification of religion was not "the words of our mouths" or the "meditations of our hearts," it was "the work of our hands." The test of faith was not creed but deed, not the world to come but fixing the here and now. *Tikkun olam* was, for him, the deepest meaning of Judaism and of faith itself.

To his political opponents and even to some of his allies, Eisendrath was a formidable, almost intimidating, personality. But there was another side to Maurice Eisendrath—a tender, caring, gentle husband; a warm, loyal, and steadfast friend and colleague. Although never blessed with children of his own, he adored children and took special pride in the Eisendrath Exchange Program, which brings Israeli youngsters to the United States for several months and sends Jewish kids from the United States to Israel for extended periods. It was fitting that perhaps his last conversation before his sudden death at the 1973 General Assembly in New York City was with a group of Israeli teenagers attending the convention as Eisendrath exchange students. Maurice was shy in private, awkward with small talk, but his few friendships were deep and enduring, as lifelong relationships with such colleagues as Roland Gittelsohn demonstrate.

Maurice Eisendrath was a bundle of contradictions. He was a lifetime pacifist, but he helped to mobilize Canadian public opinion against Hitler. He began as an anti-Zionist and ended up a fervent champion of Israel. He was childless but inspired the development of NFTY, the youth organization that became Reform's proudest jewel. He was a fierce and unbending liberal but conservative and prudish about marriage, family values, and sexuality. He didn't drink, tell dirty stories, or smoke. His sins were a fondness for chocolate, for endless alliteration in his speeches, and canoeing on the waters around his secluded island of Tamagami in Canada. His prodigy, his joyful pride, was the UAHC. His life and work were a blessing for future generations. This book will help us to understand the depth of our indebtedness to this modern-day Jeremiah and to the unquenchable fire that burned in his heart.

He was a unique person. He shaped the UAHC in his vision; he woke it up, disturbed it and shook it, and brought it, sometimes screaming and yelling, into the twentieth century. Only Isaac Mayer Wise, who created the Union, and Rabbi Alexander M. Schindler, who succeeded Maurice and who lifted the UAHC from strength to new strength, poured such genius and devotion into this organization, making it a powerful vehicle of Jewish religious identity.

We are delighted to publish this biography by Rabbi Avi Schulman, which outlines the career and views of a remarkable, iconoclastic, and visionary Jew who was touched by the sustaining spiritual force of the Hebrew prophets. Maurice Eisendrath's legacy to Reform Judaism is incalculable and undying. His life was a gift and a blessing to all of us, from generation to generation. May this book help to share that gift with a wider audience of Jews of all generations.

Albert Vorspan

LIKE A
RAGING
FIRE

INTRODUCTION

Maurice Eisendrath's hands twitched as he glanced at the three men seated with him around a small conference table. Shifting his body every few moments, the president of the Union of American Hebrew Congregations (UAHC) did not allow himself the luxury of slumping in his chair. The rigidness of their boss's body and his agitated movements were familiar signs of nervousness to the three members of Eisendrath's coordinating staff who met with him on that warm fall day in 1959. They had gathered to criticize a first draft of his "State of Our Union" speech, to be given at the 45th General Assembly of the UAHC scheduled to take place in Miami Beach that November. Eisendrath always relished the opportunity to discuss and review his biennial address with a few of his lieutenants: Al Vorspan and Rabbis Jay Kaufman and Gene Lipman. It was their task to evaluate the ideas expressed in his rough draft and to suggest ways of editing the 120-page speech. In past years he had loved the give-and-take of these sessions. Each staff member was free to speak his mind, challenging the president's ideas and honing the clarity of his language. Never had Eisendrath pulled rank on his subordinates or silenced their criticisms.

However, this time was different. The staff soon realized that Eisendrath's manner was unlike that of previous sessions. This time he was acerbic and antagonistic toward anyone who suggested a way to improve his speech; he had reached the limit of his patience on a number of issues, he was unresponsive to their requests to modify his views. For some time he had been absorbing the barbed criticisms of some Southerners in the UAHC who opposed his own and the Union's stands on civil rights. They did not want the Union president threatening their position in the South with his liberal pronouncements about the sin of segregation and the evil of racial hatred. Many Southerners felt that Eisendrath had no right to speak for them, and a number of congregations and individuals had threatened to withhold funds or leave the UAHC altogether.

Eisendrath also had encountered opposition to the proposed establishment of a Religious Action Center in Washington, D.C. Reform Jews who felt that social action was not an integral part of their Jewish identity adamantly refused to have their Union dues spent to support an institution that would make social policy statements in their names.

The draft of Eisendrath's speech seemed belligerent. He intended to berate the delegates who would be at the biennial assembly, exhort them to live up to the high ideals of peace and brotherhood expressed by the prophets of Israel. His staff members feared that the speech might alienate the biennial delegates, the lay leaders of the Reform movement who volunteered their time, serving on temple boards and the various commissions of the UAHC. The staff felt that a negative speech by the Union president could seriously affect the delegates' morale and dampen their enthusiasm and support for the movement.

At past biennials, Eisendrath's "State of Our Union" addresses had served as the highlights of the conventions. His speaking ability was unmatched. He delivered his memorized speeches in florid and alliterative phrases, describing the activities of the Union and painting a picture of the new vistas of Reform Judaism. In the past he had succeeded in rallying the delegates, uniting disparate factions.

But in 1959, Eisendrath did not want merely to depict the accomplishments of the Reform movement and exhort members to labor on behalf of its causes. He was angry at Reform Jews who opposed civil rights for blacks and who lagged in working for social justice in America. He was in no mood to accept his staff's anxious suggestions that he moderate his thundering accusations against his adversaries. The exchanges between Eisendrath and his aides grew uncharacteristically heated. Suddenly, he slammed his manuscript on the table and exclaimed, "You want me to love four thousand people. I cannot." [1]

Eisendrath held to his convictions, even when expediency dictated otherwise. While a young rabbi in Canada in the early 1930s, he assailed Zionism and advocated pacifism. Later in his career, despite heated opposition, he championed civil rights for blacks, supported international nuclear disarmament, and opposed United States involvement in Vietnam. Regarded by many as a visionary, Eisendrath transformed the Union of American Hebrew Congregations from an insignificant service association in Cincinnati into a high-profile, dynamic religious organization in New York.

Eisendrath's detractors thought of him as an egocentric headline chaser. A skilled political infighter, he fought bruising battles against his opponents, rarely retreating when he felt a principle was at stake. Eisendrath met his match only in Nelson Glueck, president of the Hebrew Union College-Jewish Institute of Religion. For more than twenty years, the two leaders competed bitterly in a struggle for supremacy within the Reform movement.

Eisendrath did not easily display emotion and he shunned idle talk. One former associate described him as politically radical but socially Victorian. He refrained from smoking and drinking and rarely cursed, permitting himself an occasional "damn" or "hell." He believed in the sanctity of marriage and disapproved privately of staff members who divorced.

Maurice Eisendrath was a man about whom people felt strongly, either positively or negatively. Though he died in 1973, today his accomplishments are largely unknown. His name conjures up vague reminiscences of a tall, crew-cut figure carrying a Torah during a Freedom March or raising his hands in resistance to the Vietnam War.

In writing this biography, I have relied upon extensive interviews with his second wife, Rita ז"ל, former and present UAHC staff members, and others who knew him. I also have reviewed Eisendrath's speeches, sermons, and writings, spanning his nearly fifty-year rabbinical career. In addition, I have examined secondary sources that have helped me better understand Eisendrath's thoughts and actions in the context of his time.

It is my hope that this biography will revive interest in a

leader who did more to shape Reform Judaism than any other person in the post–World War II period. This is not meant to be a panegyric to Eisendrath's finer qualities or a laudatory compilation of his notable achievements. It does not seek to advance the views of his detractors, but it attempts to present a fair and balanced account of the man's strengths and weaknesses.

"EISEY": 1902-1926

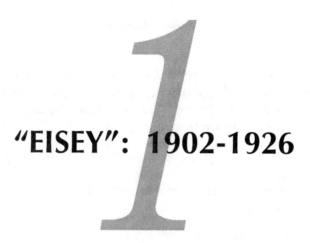

Maurice Nathan Eisendrath was born in Chicago on July 10, 1902, the second child of Clara and Nathan Eisendrath. His sister, Juliette, preceded his arrival by a few years. The Dutch branch of the Eisendrath family resided in Milwaukee; those of German descent lived in Chicago. Both Clara and Nathan, who worked in a millinery-supply business, were American-born. They made their home in a three-story flat on the North Side of Chicago and joined Temple Emanuel, a congregation then composed of German Jews. Nathan served on the temple board, and Clara often volunteered her services.

The parents sent Juliette, Maurice, and their younger brother, Arthur, to religious school at Temple Emanuel, where, through his association with Rabbi Felix Levy, Maurice decided to become a rabbi:

> I decided on a religious career when I was five, and I have never deviated. . . . It was unpopular in those days for a Reform youngster to even think of becoming a rabbi, but I couldn't be deterred. . . . I was greatly influenced by our congregation's young rabbi. He was very sympatico with children, and I admired him and wanted to be like him.

The fact that Levy was a neighbor of the Eisendraths and a close family friend reinforced Maurice's positive image of the rabbinate. Children taunted Maurice, calling him a "square" and a "sissy" for wanting to be a "do-gooder." Although his parents did not fully comprehend his early vocational desire, they never wavered in their support.

Aside from his interest in religion, Maurice was an avid baseball fan, going to games with his father and brother. He also enjoyed music, attended concerts, collected records, and played the saxophone.

Eisendrath was a frail child with a vision problem that later almost prevented him from completing rabbinic school. Marjory Hess, a childhood acquaintance, remembered Maurice "in knickers and not being able to see."

In 1914 the Eisendraths moved to Pittsburgh, where Nathan continued in the hat business. Maurice studied with J. Leonard Levy, rabbi of Congregation Rodef Shalom. Levy was famous in his day as a preacher and social activist. In later years Eisendrath remembered how this "towering figure of Reform Judaism" had influenced him.

As he grew older, Eisendrath at various times considered careers in social work, medicine, and law, yet his childhood desire to become a rabbi prevailed. In September 1918, at the age of sixteen, Maurice traveled to Cincinnati and began rabbinic studies at the Hebrew Union College (HUC).

Having had little background in Hebrew, Bible, or rabbinic literature, Maurice was one of many entering students required to enroll in the College's Preparatory Department. Within the next eight years, Eisendrath would graduate from three schools, all located on Clifton Avenue: Hughes High School, the University of Cincinnati, and Hebrew Union College.

One month after Eisendrath began his studies at HUC, his father died in an influenza epidemic. As the oldest male, Maurice felt responsible for the welfare of his family, but Clara insisted that he return to Cincinnati to continue his studies. Clara was a dominant force in her son's life. She possessed an unusually perceptive mind, and those who knew both her and

Maurice commented that he had inherited his perspicacity from her.

Eisendrath returned to HUC with renewed determination. Before completion of the HUC dormitory in 1924, students boarded with families. Despite their secular and religious studies and part-time jobs, the "boys" found time to fraternize. Student diversions included playing or rooting for the HUC basketball team, producing plays, creating Chanukah and Purim parties, and publishing a first-rate journal: the *HUC Monthly*. At that time a distinctly masculine aura pervaded the College.[1] A clear division was made between the inferior, naive, lower classmen and the more worldly, somewhat cynical, upper classmen. Like other freshmen, Eisendrath had subjected himself to a ritual induction into the student body:

> In January of 1919, at the "Students Recreation Chamber" of the College, six lowly and humble members of the freshmen class . . . were initiated into the mystic "arcana" of the HUC student body. The freshmen performed the usual vocal, lingual, and nasal antics ordinarily inflicted upon them. Everybody had a good time except the "Freshies." [2]

In time, Eisendrath adapted well to the social atmosphere of HUC. He formed a jazz band called the HUC-Stars (pronounced "hucksters"), which for several years performed at student functions. Eisendrath played saxophone and occasionally sang. At one student banquet Eisendrath regaled the crowd with a satirical song about the B.H. (Be Hutspadik) degree (actually the Bachelor of Hebrew). At another event he sang about the dilemmas of preaching on controversial subjects:

> I wish I knew what I should speak on,
>
> I wish I knew what to preach;
>
> If I should speak for labor
>
> I'd lose my job, I'd even lose my girl,
>
> The biggest *macher's* daughter.
>
> I wish I knew what I should speak on,

I wish I knew what to preach;

If I should speak on justice

I'd be a red, they'd even say I was

A wicked bol—she—vi—ki.

Eisendrath, called "Eisey" by his fellow students, adopted that nickname in a song he wrote, titled "Hot Lips," referring to his saxophone playing. Eisendrath could be quite a cutup at student parties. At one dance, according to the *HUC Monthly*, "a new style of dancing was introduced by George D. Taxay and Maurice Eisendrath—an adaptation of the Chinese 'Fang Schon on' trot and done in an inimitable way."

These social events provided the students relief from their weighty academic load. In addition to secular studies, students in the Preparatory Department took a wide array of Judaica courses taught by distinguished rabbis and scholars, including Bible (taught to Eisendrath by distinguished rabbis and scholars Moses Buttenwieser, Henry Englander, and Julian Morgenstern); rabbinic literature (by Solomon Freehof), history (by Jacob Rader Marcus), and philosophy (by David Neumark).

During his early years at the College, Eisendrath excelled in his studies. He scored particularly high marks in Bible and Mishna. In 1923 he was awarded the Fleisher Prize for his "scholarship and standing in the Preparatory Department." Later, his academic standing dropped, although he still earned good marks. In his early years Eisendrath had entertained thoughts of becoming an academician, but he lacked interest in developing the Hebrew skills necessary to become an accomplished Judaic scholar. He preferred reading the classics of English literature and the important novels of the day.

Eisendrath had difficulty reconciling his childhood belief in a paternal, personal God with the more critical, scientific perspectives to which he was exposed during his college years. Two men helped guide Eisendrath through his theological crisis. HUC Bible Professor Moses Buttenwieser, "through his unparalleled presentation of the moral passion of the Hebrew prophets," taught Eisendrath that Judaism placed greater emphasis on right conduct than on right belief. Buttenwieser also taught his doubting student that, although one could never rationally know God, one must trust in God in times of trial.

Eustace Haydon, professor of comparative religion at the University of Chicago Divinity School, also influenced Eisendrath's concept of God. It was during his summer studies in Chicago that Eisendrath abandoned his childhood perspective of God as a grandfatherly deity and adopted the view of God as an active cosmic force. Eisendrath absorbed from Haydon a lifetime faith in "that spirit which suffuses the universe—which *is*, in the literal meaning of that term, veritably a universe and not a chaos—linking the soaring satellites and flaming suns with an Amos, a Beethoven, an Abraham Lincoln, an Albert Einstein."

Eisendrath almost failed to complete his studies at HUC, although not as a result of academic deficiency or a crisis of the spirit. The College's physician maintained that Eisendrath's eyes were far too weak to cope with the strain of studying. Eisendrath despaired of achieving his goal of becoming a rabbi. Fortunately, HUC's president, Julian Morgenstern, recommended that he see the best oculist in Chicago. Dr. Snydacker diagnosed his condition as severe congenital astigmatism and advised Eisendrath to improve his general health (he was five feet eleven inches tall and weighed only 125 pounds) so as to strengthen his eyesight. Dr. Snydacker's prescription proved correct, though it cannot be said that Eisendrath applied himself assiduously to the task of body-building. He liked to swim but deliberately skipped the mandatory gym courses at the University of Cincinnati, jeopardizing his graduation. HUC President Morgenstern assured the university dean that in two weeks Eisendrath would make up four years of missed gym classes. Eisendrath later recalled the fourteen days of relentless drilling under "Coach" Morgenstern's supervision:

> My college mates of that day may still recall the side-splitting spectacle of my ceaseless running, huffing and puffing around the campus driveway or shakily raising dumbbells

in the gym until I was blue in the face, as I so belatedly discharged my athletic requirements under the tireless coaching of Dr. Morgenstern. [3]

In addition to completing academic requirements, HUC students were required to teach in nearby religious schools and to lead services at small congregations unable to afford full-time rabbis. Eisendrath received his first practical rabbinic experience in 1920, leading High Holy Day services in Fremont, Ohio. The congregation's president wrote Dr. Englander, the College registrar:

> Mr. Eisendrath conducted our services in such a highly satisfactory manner that we would very much like to have him with us again next year if possible. He certainly has a wonderful future.

As a student, Eisendrath also conducted High Holy Day services in Helena, Montana; Muskogee, Oklahoma; and Butte, Montana. During his last two years at HUC he was assigned a biweekly pulpit in Owensboro, Kentucky. Muskogee, Oklahoma, one of Eisendrath's student pulpits, was the hometown of his first wife, Rosa Brown. An accomplished pianist, Rosa studied music at the University of Chicago, where she roomed with Maurice's sister, Juliette. Rose and Maurice dated for several years, but postponed marriage until Maurice finished his studies.

Like many of his colleagues, Eisendrath responded passionately to the prophetic call for social justice. In Reform Judaism, the Hebrew prophets came to represent the living ethical spirit of Judaism, in contrast to the decadent performance of rote rituals. Given this preoccupation with prophetic ideals, HUC students tended to portray any conflicts with authority figures at the College as a struggle between the sons of light and the fathers of darkness.

A variety of factors contributed to the confrontational mood that prevailed in 1925 between students and Dr. Julian Morgenstern. Many students resented his aloof manner and occasional heavy-handed discipline, his favoritism toward certain students, and his lowering of admission standards at the

College while insisting on higher academic standards for the student body.

In his essay, "The Supremacy of Self," published in the February 1925 issue of the *HUC Monthly*, Eisendrath argued that the true molders of civilization opposed the unholy doctrine of conformity and called for a breaking-away from the masses to express a new and exalted vision of the self. Across the world, lamented Eisendrath, individuality was being stamped out. "Strange as it may seem," he wrote, "this all pervading darkness has spread its ominous gloom even to religious institutions and theological seminaries. Any deviations from the standard rule of conduct or thought might even render one in imminent need of psychiatric attention or at least of a rigorous regimen of gymnastics. It would take brave souls to assert themselves against the elders who attempted to impose their false beliefs upon the young. Respect for authority is not always laudable. It may be necessary to rebel against tyranny. It is better to renounce those who guide a vessel than to perish amid icy waves because of the pilot's ineptitude."

Eisendrath said later that as a "restive and rebellious student" he had led a revolt to remove Dr. Morgenstern because of the president's attempt to impose discipline. Yet, curiously, Eisendrath chose to write his rabbinic thesis ("Universalism and Particularism in the Priestly Code with Special Reference to Ezekiel and Deutero-Isaiah") under the man he once had passionately denounced! Perhaps Eisendrath's conflict with Morgenstern prompted a special understanding between the two. Or perhaps Eisendrath sought to curry favor with the College president. In those days, before the establishment of the Placement Commission of the Central Conference of American Rabbis, the College president had great influence over postordination job placements. [4]

Eisendrath's approach to his thesis material was unoriginal but accepted. His thesis sought to trace the rise and interplay of the twin Jewish doctrines of particularism and universalism. He outlined how Israel's religious history gradually progressed from narrow particularism toward the universalism of Deutero-Isaiah. After the "night of nationalism," he wrote, came "the dawn . . . of universal moral ideals." Israel would become a light unto the nations. As God's suffering servant, Israel would become by example a teacher of humanity.

Eisendrath completed his thesis in May 1926. By the end of his college days he seemed eager to leave the cloistered halls of HUC. In his senior sermon he expressed his feelings about entering the active rabbinate:

> With anchor weighed, adrift upon an unchartered sea, we too must set out for that shore, unnamed in any atlas, that shore which may never be attained; but in the sailing forth, in the sheer joy of having cast off from our earthly moorings . . . in this alone can we satisfy the undying desire of the soul to fulfill itself, of the spirit, craving for completeness of life, yearning, ever striving to surpass itself.

Eisendrath entered the Hebrew Union College a young lad of sixteen and emerged eight years later an adult, yet he never lost his penchant for challenging entrenched authorities, drawing upon the prophets for inspiration.

PULPIT AND POLITICS: 1926-1943

In the fall of 1926, Eisendrath began his duties as rabbi of the Virginia Street Temple of Charleston, West Virginia. Though only two hundred miles from Cincinnati, the twenty-four-year-old must have felt very remote from the center of American Reform Judaism. West Virginia, "The Mountain State," had never been settled by a sizable number of Jews. In the nineteenth century, it was primarily an agricultural center, and few Jews were attracted to farming. In time, the state's coal industry grew in importance, but few Jews cared to work the mines. By the 1920s, only eight thousand of West Virginia's one-and-a-half million residents were Jews.

When Eisendrath arrived in Charleston, the capital of West Virginia, there were about twelve hundred Jews living in a city of fifty-one thousand. Of those Jews in the city who were affiliated, the majority associated with the Reform congregation, while a smaller number belonged to the Orthodox synagogue. The Virginia Street Temple, founded in 1873 as the Hebrew Educational Society, became the first West Virginia congregation to affiliate with the newly founded Union of American Hebrew Congregations.

Several months after taking his pulpit in Charleston, Eisendrath married Rosa Brown. For the next two years he busied himself tending to the everyday duties of the congregation and actively representing the Jews in the general community. Eisendrath soon became a regular speaker on the Rotary and Lions circuits, but he was not content to utter mere banalities of goodwill and brotherhood.

In the fall of 1928, the young rabbi took a forceful and vocal stand on a controversial issue of the day. Al Smith, governor of New York and a Catholic, was running for president against Herbert Hoover. Smith's religion became a major campaign issue, especially in West Virginia, settled predominantly by Protestant immigrants. [1] One Friday evening in October, Eisendrath delivered a sermon entitled "Shall a Roman Catholic Become President of the United States?" A standing-room-only audience of Jews and Christians heard him express his belief that if Americans truly believed in liberty, they would not oppose a presidential candidate because of his religion.

The next day, Eisendrath's sermon made front-page news in Charleston. The full text appeared in the local paper, thrusting his board of trustees into an uncomfortable position. While some congregants upheld the principle of "freedom of the pulpit," others were uneasy about their rabbi's championing an unpopular stand on an issue that could threaten the status of Charleston's Jewish minority. Despite the temple board's discomfort, Eisendrath accepted an offer from the state's Democratic committee to stump for Smith.

Years later he recalled the public reaction to a campaign speech he delivered in the public square of a small West Virginia town:

> A large crowd had already gathered, some out of curiosity, for few, if any, had ever seen a rabbi . . . . Every face before us stared sullen, stolid, stony. Every lapel was adorned with a Hoover button. My wife, . . . for the first and only time, requested that I delete a passage from an address. She whispered the suggestion that I might omit my peroration wherein I stated that "If I had to choose between being ruled by the Pope of Rome or the Grand Kleagle of the Ku Klux Klan . . . I would choose the Pope of Rome."

Eisendrath gave the speech in its entirety, Pope of Rome,

Grand Kleagle, and all. In later years he would reflect that the brashness of youth and his naive certainty that he could help usher in the Kingdom of God compelled him to face hostile crowds. Unlike others who mellowed considerably as they grew older, Eisendrath lost neither his prophetic zeal nor his penchant for embracing controversial positions.

In 1929, Eisendrath accepted the position of rabbi of Holy Blossom Temple of Toronto, Canada. That he was chosen to be the sole rabbi of a large congregation at the age of twenty-seven attests to his drive, ambition, and skill. During his years in Charleston, he had gone on occasional speaking tours, which to some degree helped him hone his oratorical abilities. But there must have been something special about the young man that impressed the temple's board of trustees. He was perceived as a "comer," the kind of man the board sought—one who would grow and develop with the congregation. They would not be disappointed.

Eisendrath realized quickly how significantly Canada differed from the United States. The "melting pot" concept was alien to Canadians, who showed greater tolerance for ethnic diversity. The tension between Canadian French Catholics and Anglo Protestants mitigated against a single cultural identity. Canadian Jews differed as well, identifying more closely with the Old World than did their cousins in the United States. At the turn of the century, only 15,000 Jews resided in Canada. By 1914, that number had increased about sevenfold to 100,000. The Canada that Eisendrath came to know had a Jewish population of about 150,000, [2] with approximately one-third living in Toronto and another third in Montreal. Canadian Jews tended to speak more Yiddish in the home, provide a more thorough Jewish education for their young, contribute more per capita to Jewish causes, and favor an Orthodox congregation. They also were more supportive of Zionism than were American Jews.

Unlike the prominence of Reform Judaism in the United States, the liberal movement in Canada was virtually unknown. A survey conducted in 1935 found 152 Jewish congregations in all of Canada: 140 were Orthodox, 9

Conservative, 3 Reform (formerly Orthodox). Holy Blossom was the oldest, founded in 1856. Its metamorphosis from Orthodox to Reform took decades. The auctioning of Torah honors was forbidden in the 1880s; mixed family pews were introduced in the 1920s, the same decade during which the congregation joined the UAHC.

Prior to settling in Toronto, Eisendrath became a contributing editor to the *Canadian Jewish Review*. In his first editorial, "We Pacifists," he voiced support for the creation of a binational state in Palestine. His editorial rocked Canadian Jewish leaders, who found his views inconceivable, especially in light of recent Arab riots. In certain Jewish quarters he was labeled a *mamzer* and a *meshummed* (a bastard and a traitor). Canadian Zionists, including the president of Hadassah, demanded that Holy Blossom dismiss Eisendrath, but the temple's board refused. A few weeks after the controversial editorial, Eisendrath shocked his congregants when he became the first Holy Blossom rabbi to lead High Holy Day services without wearing a head covering.

Throughout his fourteen-year tenure as rabbi of Holy Blossom Temple, Eisendrath promoted himself, in part, by utilizing the temple bulletin to a degree unknown by his predecessors. The bulletin gave his home address and phone number with the occasional reminder that, despite the rabbi's busy schedule, he was always available for pastoral visits. The *Holy Blossom Bulletin* regularly contained a preview of the upcoming Sunday sermon, which typically concerned "urgent problems" of "worldwide proportion." (In the early decades of this century, the principal service of many large Reform temples in North America was held on Sunday morning.)

Through the bulletin, Eisendrath kept his congregants informed about his communal activities, including his extensive speaking engagements. In the course of a week it was not unusual for the rabbi to speak at six or seven different public events, many of them Christian sponsored. For instance, the February 12, 1931, *Holy Blossom Bulletin* states:

> Rabbi Eisendrath has recently addressed the St. Paul's
> United Church in Brampton; the Student's Christian

Association at Hart House; the Y.M.C.A.; the First United
Church and the Wesley United Church in Galt, Ontario;
and the Men's Club of Parkdale United Church in Toronto.

His "Rabbi in the Community" column often included words
of tribute, such as the following assessment of his pioneering
visit to the Christian Church in Ottawa:

> Rabbi Eisendrath, a brilliant Hebrew scholar, preacher and
> writer, held the large congregation absolutely silent for half
> an hour or more while he spoke on "If I Were a Christian."
> Every seat was filled, scores stood in the doorways, around
> the walls, in the corridors, vestry and choir room . . . wher-
> ever a spot could be found to hear the noted Rabbi.
>
> Long before the hour of service, the great auditorium
> was filled. . . . In the congregation were representatives of
> every race and creed, including many of the Hebrew faith
> who had been specially invited by the minister of St. James.

Eisendrath's eloquent Sunday sermons drew large crowds of
congregants and Gentiles alike. He crafted his sermons with
care, demonstrating great oratorical skill and a broad familiar-
ity with Jewish and non-Jewish sources. He memorized every
speech, amazing his listeners with his vivid prose. He relied
on a blend of reason and subtle emotion to move his audiences.
His impact upon non-Jewish listeners can scarcely be imagined
today. Here was an educated man, a Jew well versed in the
Bible but also conversant with world literature. He was a
handsome and proud man who seemed in every way completely modern. And when his elegant, inspiring addresses appealed
to the shared spiritual heritage of Christian and Jew, his non-
Jewish listeners must have been tremendously impressed.

Eisendrath became the first Canadian rabbi to host a
national radio program—"Forum on the Air." His half-hour
addresses were broadcast weekly from coast to coast, publiciz-
ing his religious action agenda: "If Jewish tradition teaches us
anything at all, it teaches us that religion must dominate the
whole of life; that politics and economics must all be subject to
its supreme and absolute command . . . . If religion is to survive at all, . . . then it must storm the very citadels of political

power and economic might with its spiritual preachment and moral protest until society be no longer organized for the impoverishment of the many and the enrichment of the few. For it is utterly futile to suppose that the spiritual life can flourish in such an environment . . . . One cannot call himself after the name of Moses or Amos or Jeremiah and fail, even through political action, to battle for the rights of man and for the establishment of the kingdom of righteousness on earth."

Eisendrath was not content to preach ethics; he was a forceful activist. In Toronto he condemned the attempt to close Queens Park, which was the Canadian equivalent of London's Hyde Park. He also drew attention to the squalid living conditions of some city residents. In 1936 he was invited by the lieutenant governor to become a member of the Executive Committee of the Housing Centre, the agency charged with slum clearance and housing development.

A self-described "absolute and dogmatic pacifist," Eisendrath harbored a lifelong revulsion to physical violence of any kind. He was firmly convinced that one must not fight fire with fire. "On the contrary," he argued, "one fights fire with water." In a 1931 sermon he railed against those who relied upon might to achieve their ambitions:

> The Hebrew prophets, Jesus, and the persecuted martyrs of Rome knew long centuries ago that the real enemy of man was not this tribe or clan or nation, but this reliance upon sword and spear and force and fortress. They knew that, while the chariots of Egypt and the horsemen of Assyria might triumph for the hour, in the end all those who place their trust in military alliances would themselves be destroyed thereby. They anticipated by many centuries the inescapable truth . . . that our true foe today is not this people or that but the war system itself.

Soon after his arrival in Toronto, Eisendrath helped establish a local chapter of the Fellowship of Reconciliation, an international organization advocating nonviolence. In the summer of 1931, Maurice and Rosa attended an international conference of the fellowship in Holland and, later that year, organized a well-attended disarmament rally in Toronto.

The rise of the German National Socialist Party forced Eisendrath to reconsider his cherished ideals of nonviolence. After visiting Germany in 1931 and 1933, he acknowledged the perils of National Socialism to Jews and to all humanity. In "Who Is 'The Chosen People'?" one in a series of anti-Nazi sermons, he said,

> And if you be not politically naive . . . you will behold in the rise of National Socialism in Germany not a passing storm but the torrential tempest of an ego-intoxicated regime convinced that to it alone hath been given the right to dominate the whole of humankind.

> What all this means for the future of our world; just how soon this delirious dream of the chosen German people may plunge us into another catastrophic war, no man would dare to prophesy.

Eisendrath returned to Germany in 1935 and 1936. After each visit he sought to alert Canadians to the growing Nazi danger, but encountered widespread indifference.

In 1937 the Canadian government backed British efforts to appease Hitler. That same year the number of anti-Semitic incidents in Canada increased. [3] On Halloween, Eisendrath found a swastika and funeral shroud nailed to his front door. "What happened on my doorstep is of little moment," he told the press, "but what is happening throughout Canada is vitally significant." A month later, Eisendrath prompted the press to investigate the activities of the Canadian Nazi party.

As the condition of Jews worsened in Europe, Eisendrath committed himself to alleviating their plight. The Canadian government proved uncooperative, virtually closing its borders to Jewish immigration. From 1933 to 1939 Canada found room for only four thousand Jewish refugees. [4] Eisendrath's efforts from the pulpit and as a member of the Canadian Jewish Congress Refugee Committee failed to persuade government officials to loosen the nation's immigration policy.

When Canada entered the war, the young idealist assented reluctantly. His anguished reflections upon the "dilemmas of a pacifist" are portrayed in an essay of the same title written in 1964.

While some Canadians shared Eisendrath's pacifism in the early 1930s, they rejected his views on Zionism. Typical of most Reform Jews of his era, Eisendrath had been reared in a household and attended a temple that were hostile to Zionism. Jewish colonization of the ancient Jewish homeland was of little concern for Diaspora Jews concerned with being a "light unto the nations." While at the Hebrew Union College, Eisendrath shared the anti-Zionist convictions of the majority of professors and students, opposing the creation of a Jewish national entity in Palestine. In 1934, Eisendrath went so far as to compare some Zionists to Nazis:

> A Jewish National state is what they seek, and he who would call a halt to this fulfillment of our enemies' most malicious libel is called a traitor; he who would concentrate our splendid Jewish energies upon what is ofttimes sneeringly dubbed "the mission of Israel," upon the building of a more decent homeland for *all* the children of men, is regarded—almost the very words of the Nazis themselves are sometimes used by the more odious of these Jewish jingoes—as sabotaging Israel's nationalistic dreams.

> That is the concept against which some of us must continue to protest, even if we be made to stand alone contra mundum. That this vision of Jewish national rebirth, whether in Palestine or the Diaspora, has kindled new enthusiasm in Jewish life, especially among our Jewish youth; that Jewish cultural and spiritual activities are deserted while mass meetings are swarming with Jewish young men and women, is beside the point. Churches are likewise struggling for existence while youthful storm troopers or komsomols parade in endless battalions throughout their respective lands. Fascism appeals to youth. Communism appeals to youth. Hitlerism appeals magnificently to youth, and so does Jewish nationalism. Which only makes it quite as dangerous to the essential spirit of

the Jew as Fascism, Communism and Hitlerism are to the essence of Christianity.

Eisendrath came to regret this vitriolic statement, for later he would support to some degree the goals of Zionism. How much his view of Zionism changed is open to question. Eisendrath himself claimed that he underwent a radical transformation during his first visit to Palestine in 1935. Through contact with Labor Zionist leaders such as David Ben-Gurion, Moshe Sharett, Zalman Shazar, and Golda Meir—and through exposure to *kibbutzim and moshavim*—he felt "reborn" as a committed friend of Palestine. Upon his return, he devoted a number of sermons to praising the efforts in Zion to rebuild the Jewish Commonwealth.

In a 1936 sermon he expressed admiration for the *chalutzim* (pioneers), not so much for reclaiming the Land of Israel, but for the example they set for Jewish youth in the West:

> Instead of placing our trust in political programs and revolutionary propaganda, our miserably exploited toilers might likewise band together and begin themselves to build a better and more comradely life. Especially our youth . . . might well emulate the example of those youthful pioneers of Zion, set out upon some such cooperative quest even in the midst of our capitalist and competitive economy.

But the Zionist effort was viewed from afar. Eisendrath was firmly committed to fostering Jewish life in the Diaspora. After 1936 he rarely commented on Palestine in his sermons. His trip to Palestine seems to have been the highpoint of his infatuation with the pioneers of Zion.

Jewish-Christian dialogue, however, remained an intense lifelong involvement. Eisendrath established cordial relations with clergymen of all Christian denominations, including the United Church's G. Stanley Russell, Claris E. Silcox, and Gordon Sisco. Silcox and Eisendrath participated in founding the first Jewish-Gentile seminar held in Canada, forerunner of the Canadian Conference of Christians and Jews.

In 1937 Eisendrath and the Reverand E. Crossley Hunter

embarked on a goodwill tour of Ontario towns and hamlets. Eisendrath spoke on the "spiritual purpose of Christianity" while Hunter extolled Jewish contributions to Canadian life.

One Christian publication commented:

We have seldom seen a mixed audience so deeply moved. . . . It brought a new vision to the minds of those present. The Jews were most enthusiastic; several of them said that they had never heard a Christian minister before. The atmosphere of the meeting was that of worship at its highest point.

By the mid-1930s, Eisendrath was firmly established as a leader of Canadian Jewry. Widely known by Jews both in Canada and in the United States, he was viewed as a man on the move. Although he frequently left Toronto for speaking tours or study trips abroad, he faithfully attended to his congregational duties. In the *Holy Blossom Bulletin,* the president of Holy Blossom Temple wrote of the rabbi's manifold responsibilities.

The Rabbi must visit all the families of his flock; bring comfort to all the sick and afflicted; participate in all social functions of the congregation; superintend the religious school; organize classes of all kinds; assist the Sisterhood and Brotherhood; make speeches on every occasion; mingle constantly with non-Jewish organizations to maintain goodwill; attend the meetings of the Welfare Fund, Canadian Jewish Congress, Housing Committee, Toronto Symphony Orchestra Association, National Conference of Christians and Jews, our own Board of Trustees; address service clubs; speak in churches; conduct Sabbath morning services; deliver an inspiring and breath-taking sermon every Sunday morning; and so I could go on almost endlessly.

Rosa was to Maurice a devoted helpmate and close confidante. The career-oriented rabbi and his protective wife chose to remain childless. She often reviewed or edited his speeches and sermons and frequently traveled with him. If someone dared to criticize her husband, Rosa would rise to his defense.

One ambition Eisendrath harbored from the moment he arrived in Toronto was to build a new and larger Holy Blossom Temple. In 1936, in the midst of the Depression, he convinced the board to realize a decade-old dream of the congregation—to move from Bond Street in a dilapidated neighborhood of downtown Toronto to a northern suburb of the city. The dedication of the new temple on Bathurst Street on May 20, 1938, was attended by the governor general of Canada and by Eisendrath's former Hebrew Union College professor of Bible, Dr. Julian Morgenstern, who was also president of the College.

In the fall of 1939 Maurice and Rosa were feted at Holy Blossom Temple for a decade of service. His collection of sermons, *The Never Failing Stream*, appeared the same year. Eisendrath could have remained at Holy Blossom for another thirty or forty years, gaining ever greater influence and stature as a leader of Canadian Jewry. However, as one associate observed, "Eisendrath desperately wanted to get out of Holy Blossom. He was a very ambitious man. He wanted to be a great man. There was a fire that raged within him." [5]

In 1943, a position opened that offered him the potential for enhanced prestige and influence. He agreed to become the interim director of the Union of American Hebrew Congregations, a move that would change the course of Reform Judaism in North America.

AT THE UNION'S HELM: 1943-1951

In the early 1940s the Union of American Hebrew Congregations was located on a floor and a half of the modest Merchants Building on Sixth Street in downtown Cincinnati. Few took the organization seriously; it was overshadowed by the Hebrew Union College. Maurice Eisendrath would forge the Union into a significant force in American Jewish life.

In order to understand Eisendrath's impact as leader of the Union of American Hebrew Congregations, one must understand that prior to Eisendrath, there were no Union camps, outreach or social justice programs, regional directors, or national departments. Nor was the Union located in its current headquarters in New York in the House of Living Judaism.

Since the mid-nineteenth century, Rabbi Isaac Mayer Wise had labored to organize a national organization of American Israelites. Wise dreamed of uniting every Jew in America, but regional and personal rivalries interfered. In 1873 a group of Cincinnati Jews, led by Moritz Loth, succeeded in attracting to Cincinnati representatives from congregations in the West and the South. On July 8, 1873, delegates from thirty-four congregations inaugurated the Union of American Hebrew Congregations in its first convention. They set forth as their primary objective the founding of a Hebrew theological institute. Each congregation would contribute one dollar annually per member to fund the Union. For every twenty-five congregational members, one representative would be sent to the Union council, which would meet periodically to set policies. The UAHC would be run by an executive board composed of members elected by the council.

The organization's first goal—establishing a school to "preserve Judaism intact, to bequeath it in its purity and sublimity to posterity" [1]—was promptly achieved. The Hebrew Union College opened its doors in 1875. Isaac Mayer Wise served as its president for twenty-five years.

In its formative years, the Union functioned primarily as a fund-raising instrument for Hebrew Union College. Lipman Levy, the first staff member of the Union, conducted the organization's business from his Cincinnati law office. Early plans for the Union to provide resources for Sabbath schools and to assist in the growth of young congregations remained unfulfilled.

In 1910, Rabbi George Zepin became the full-time secretary of the UAHC. He worked tirelessly to develop and promote the Union. Historian Jacob Rader Marcus has described Zepin as a "brilliant organizer who had a broad vision of a Union embracing all of American Judaism." He helped establish the National Federation of Temple Sisterhoods (NFTS), the National Federation of Temple Brotherhoods (NFTB), and the National Federation of Temple Youth (NFTY), and coordinated the Union's efforts to work with B'nai B'rith in establishing organizations for Jewish students on college campuses. Zepin also recruited circuit preachers for the benefit of Jews in remote areas of the country. During this period the Union's department of education, under the able direction of Dr. Emanuel Gamoran, became a leading innovator in the field of Jewish instruction.

Despite Zepin's innovations, the Union stagnated from the late 1920s through the 1930s, with few congregations joining and the total number of new members increasing by only 2,000 from 1926 to 1937. The Depression unquestionably affected congregational and Union membership, but according to historian Sefton D. Temkin, a second factor may have been even more significant:

> To a large extent the successes and limitations of the
> Union . . . largely reflected [Zepin's] personality. Zepin
> was a model civil servant, wholly devoted to his duties, self-
> effacing, firm in his belief that it was his duty to guide and
> support his elected officers, and that the elected officers
> were entitled not only to take the decisions, but to appear to
> the world as having taken them. He had many ideas but
> lacked the ability to inspire his officers to take action on
> them.

In the late 1930s, the Union was unable to raise sufficient operating funds, prompting the formation of a survey committee to study the organization's effectiveness. In 1941 the committee made its report before the Union council. Rabbi Louis Mann of Chicago presented a scathing condemnation of the Union. His address, later entitled "While the Union Slept," noted the UAHC's failure to raise money, to take over the sponsorship of the campus Hillels, to use the media effectively, and to be taken seriously by anti-defamation activists. Mann indicated that the social prominence and financial security of many Reform leaders promoted complacency and prevented the Union from meeting the challenges of the day. Mann's suggestions to resolve these problems were direct: retire the professional staff and shake up the executive board.

Zepin had submitted his resignation before the Union council convened, but he probably did not anticipate the fury of Rabbi Mann's attack. Dr. Jane Evans, then executive director of NFTS, later characterized "While the Union Slept" as "a very cruel speech which, despite its intentions, amounted to a public excoriation of Zepin's life work."

Rabbi Edward Israel of Baltimore succeeded Zepin in 1941. A dynamic figure, Rabbi Israel championed the cause of the working person, ardently supported Zionism, served as a member of the American Jewish Congress and the World Jewish Congress, and was a former president of the Synagogue

Council of America. His selection indicated the executive board's desire to install someone with prestige and influence in the Jewish community, someone who could raise morale and funds and set the Union in motion.

Edward Israel requested that he be hired as the director, not as secretary of the Union. A resolution drafted by Adolph Rosenberg, then president of the executive board, provided that "he [Israel] may be given any other title at any time which is agreed upon between himself and the executive board." This was a precedent-setting resolution, enabling Eisendrath later to assume the title of president of the Union.

Edward Israel also initiated a process that Eisendrath would later complete when he proposed that the Union relocate from Cincinnati. For years the Union had its headquarters in the Merchants Building at 32 West 6th Street. Jane Evans recalled the offices as a cluster of "unpretentious little cubbyholes with one big workroom in the back." Rabbi Eugene Borowitz, then a rabbinic student who worked part-time at the Union, described the Union headquarters as follows:

> It gave you the sense . . . that this was a very old-fashioned, small, dowdy outfit. It was a series of little custodial warrens in which certain rabbits took care of their little duties. . . . [There was] a sense of Germanic prudence . . . and bureaucratic self-protection and stuffiness.

Edward Israel was convinced that in order for the Union to gain strength and prestige, it could not remain centered in Cincinnati. "We of the UAHC," he once said, "have 'missed the boat' because we weren't at the point from which boats were sailing." A great deal of opposition arose to the relocation idea because of sentimental attachment to Cincinnati as the cradle of the Reform movement. Some objected to the allocation of funds needed for the move; others insisted the budget required for operating in New York would decrease, not increase, funds for programs to benefit congregations.

A special board committee recommended that the director be authorized to open an office of the Union in Washington, D.C. The nation's capital had been Edward Israel's choice because of Washington's importance in the nation's life and because of his extensive contacts in Baltimore, where he had served as a congregational rabbi. Tragically, Edward Israel never lived to see his vision realized. In October of 1941, just three months after assuming office, he died of a heart attack suffered as he rose to speak during his first Union executive board meeting as the organization's professional head.

The Union selected as his replacement Dr. Nelson Glueck, professor of Bible and biblical archaeology at HUC. Glueck was the "fair-haired boy of America" in Dr. Marcus's phrase. He had a growing international reputation as a scholar. Handsome, regal, and dignified, Glueck possessed charm and charisma. Though he had little congregational experience, he so impressed the Union board that it agreed to allow him to retain his professorial post.

At the time, the country was involved in World War II. Before Glueck began his term at the Union, the Office of Strategic Services (O.S.S.) called upon him to undertake espionage work in the Middle East. [2] The Union's executive board granted Glueck a leave of absence. As a result, the organization was without effective leadership for the second half of 1942. It was a troubled time for the Union and the Reform movement. George Zepin's resignation, Edward Israel's death, and Nelson Glueck's departure all had occurred within a year. It was also a time when the Reform movement wrestled with the divisive issue of Zionism. The 1942 convention of the Central Conference of American Rabbis passed a resolution endorsing the formation of a Jewish army in Palestine. Anti-Zionist Reform rabbis responded by forming the American Council for Judaism, which emphasized the religious nature of Judaism in opposition to Zionism's political thrust.

The American Council for Judaism provoked bitter debate within both the CCAR and the UAHC, which had a number of ACJ supporters on their boards. The Zionism debate gained urgency as atrocities against European Jewry escalated.

Glueck's indeterminable absence prompted the Union's leaders to engage an interim director. In January 1943, Maurice Eisendrath was selected for the position and, nine months later, he replaced Nelson Glueck as UAHC director.

There are two plausible interpretations of Eisendrath's selection to be the interim and then the permanent director of the Union. The first might be called the "manipulation theory." This hypothesis assumes that Maurice Eisendrath was a very ambitious and shrewd man. Having accomplished much in Toronto, he was looking for broader horizons. During the course of his fourteen years at Holy Blossom Temple he had established himself as a leading spokesman for Reform Judaism in Canada and the United States. He was very active and well connected in the Reform movement, faithfully attending the biennials of the UAHC. In the late 1930s he was a member on the CCAR's Social Justice Commission, as well as serving on the HUC Board.

Eisendrath had been the selection committee's second choice to succeed Edward Israel. The "manipulation theory" assumes that as soon as Eisendrath became the interim director of the Union, he sought to depose Glueck. Jacob R. Marcus recalled with indignation how Eisendrath had attempted to have him convince Glueck, a close friend, to resign.

Another possible interpretation, which can be called the "reluctant bridegroom theory," holds that the ambitious Glueck, who lacked any vision of the Union's future, took the job as director to enhance his reputation. When the opportunity arose to undertake a mission for the O.S.S., Glueck willingly accepted.

Given the various grave challenges facing the Reform movement, the Union's leadership sought a temporary replacement for Glueck. Eisendrath was approached informally by Jane Evans of the National Federation of Temple Sisterhoods, who inquired discreetly if he would be interested in the UAHC position and encouraged him to consider it. Dr. Evans recalls that it was with some reluctance that he left his pulpit in Toronto because the congregation had a new building and his future as a leader of Canadian Jewry looked promising.[3] However, Eisendrath believed it was his duty to Reform Judaism to fill in for Glueck. He also felt that the move would enhance his career.

It became apparent to Adolph Rosenberg, president of the UAHC, to Solomon Freehof, president of the CCAR, and to Julian Morgenstern, the president of the Hebrew Union College, "that the Union could not be directed by remote control. There were too many crises for American Judaism and there was a need for a hands-on director." [4]

In late August 1943, Glueck was told that the Union was in dire need of a permanent director. Glueck indicated that his first duty was to the United States, which had assigned him to a tour of duty in Palestine. Two weeks later Glueck tendered his resignation.

At the next meeting of the executive board, on October 3, 1943, Adolph Rosenberg read the letter of resignation and indicated that Glueck had expressed no regrets about stepping down. Robert Goldman, past president of the Union, added that Glueck had endorsed Eisendrath's nomination to become full-time director, after which Eisendrath was elected unanimously to take the reins of the Union. It is open to interpretation whether Eisendrath actually maneuvered to obtain the director's post or whether he reluctantly agreed to succeed Glueck. Possibly a combination of both theories is correct. What is indisputable is the fact that, following Eisendrath's selection as permanent director, the relationship between Eisendrath and Glueck deteriorated.

The Zionist debate demanded much of Eisendrath's attention during the first years of his administration. He recognized the need to provide a place of refuge for Jews but strongly disagreed with those who declared that only in Zion could Jews be redeemed. Eisendrath's foremost institutional concern was the widening gulf between supporters and opponents of the American Council for Judaism.

Subscribing to Abraham Lincoln's maxim that "a divided house cannot stand," Eisendrath advocated a moderate position that restored unity in the movement, aligning the Union with the mainstream American Jewish position on the Zionism question. To achieve this goal, he promoted UAHC participation in the American Jewish Conference, a gathering of more than five hundred delegates representing some sixty national Jewish organizations that coordinated efforts on behalf of the Jews of Europe and Palestine. Some UAHC leaders feared that the American Jewish Conference might pursue a pro-Zionist policy opposed by many Reform Jews. Aided by a special committee of rabbis and laity, Eisendrath conceived a compromise proposal. It stipulated that the Union would participate in the American Jewish Conference, but all AJC resolutions would have to be approved by the Union's executive board.

When the American Jewish Conference passed a resolution calling for unlimited immigration into Palestine and the re-creation of the Jewish Commonwealth, several members of the Union delegation threatened to walk out. They relented after Eisendrath and others persuaded them that to do so would cause irreparable harm to the UAHC's standing in the American Jewish community.

The "Palestine Resolution" of the American Jewish Conference was debated at the October 3, 1943, meeting of the Union's executive board. [5] Concerned that an endorsement of the resolution might split the movement, Eisendrath asked that the ratification vote be postponed until the 1946 biennial. The board agreed reluctantly. A month later, Eisendrath felt compelled to call a meeting in Cincinnati of a number of Reform rabbis who had issued a statement urging individual congregants to determine their own attitude on the Palestine Resolution. The Union itself would remain neutral.

Rabbi Abba Hillel Silver, a fervent Reform Zionist, attacked Eisendrath bitterly for having been "intimidated by the determined opposition within the executive board." Silver attributed the Union's failure to adopt the Palestine Resolution to Eisendrath's "blundering and inconsistencies."

Howard Greenstein sums up Eisendrath's dilemma in *Turning Point: Zionism and Reform Judaism*:

> In addition to the verbal assault from militant Zionists like Silver, Eisendrath also endured bitter recriminations from other colleagues and laymen who resented the activities of

all "extremists" and urged Eisendrath to state clearly and unequivocally the neutrality of the Union on this whole issue. He was criticized for acting too aggressively and not aggressively enough. He was caught on both horns of a dilemma—moderation infuriated extremists in both camps, while extremism infuriated the moderates. [6]

During the debate over the Palestine Resolution, a controversy erupted within Houston's Congregation Beth Israel. At issue was whether Robert Kahn, the assistant rabbi and a Zionist, would succeed the retiring senior rabbi. Instead, the anti-Zionist majority hired Hyman Schachtel, a classical Reform rabbi and founding member of the American Council for Judaism. Forced by the opposition to defend their choice of senior rabbi, the congregation's board felt obliged to articulate a precise definition of the "true principles of Judaism." Their formulation essentially restated the Pittsburgh Platform of 1885, dismissing the Columbus Platform of 1937, which affirmed the "obligation of all Jewry to aid in [Palestine's] upbuilding as a Jewish homeland." Congregation Beth Israel sought to identify itself as part of a religious community, rejecting Jewish nationalism. They neither prayed for nor hoped for a return to Zion.

Beth Israel then instituted a two-class membership system; supporters of the congregation's ideological stance could vote, while those who dissented, including a number of new members of East European background, could not. The board's move to restrict members' rights on the basis of their beliefs sparked a national controversy. Eisendrath sought a meeting with Beth Israel's board but was rebuffed.

On January 18, 1944, the Union's executive board voted to repudiate the Houston congregation for adopting an exclusionist membership policy. Eisendrath agreed with the repudiation but was confronted with the conflict of balancing national authority with local autonomy of congregations. Each congregation reserved the right to determine and uphold its interpretations of Judaism. Eisendrath also felt concern about the potential negative publicity of the controversy: the Houston episode focused the attention of non-Reform Jews on the rift within the movement over Zionism and over the basic principles of Reform Judaism.

Ironically, Congregation Beth Israel's unbending adherence to the principles of classical Judaism may have accelerated a rapprochement between Reform Judaism and Zionism. As Howard Greenstein asserts, the magnitude of opposition to the American Council for Judaism and to Congregation Beth Israel

> dramatized as nothing else could, how outmoded and irrelevant the position of earlier Reform Judaism had become on the issue of Jewish nationalism, which was extremely difficult to defend any longer. It was an increasingly lonely task; and with polarization intensifying between the two sides, Reform laymen may now have found it far more comfortable to support the majority of their rabbis and lay spokesmen: and that meant an endorsement of Zionist objectives. [7]

At the 39th council session of the UAHC, held in Cincinnati in March 1946, Eisendrath denounced any attempt to establish a Reform dogma, be it anti-or pro-Zionist. He was determined that Reform Judaism reflect a dynamic American Jewish faith encompassing opposing viewpoints. He proclaimed, "We shall not regard as traitorous to Reform—or as irreligious or un-American—those among us who uphold the Zionist philosophy; not as un-Jewish those who do not."

After the Zionist issue was thoroughly debated by the delegates, the council endorsed a resolution allowing the Union to remain uncommitted on the Palestine Resolution, while maintaining membership in the American Jewish Conference. Eisendrath had achieved his objective: internal harmony while maintaining an active role in the organizational mainstream of American Judaism. He remained a member of the presidium of the American Jewish Conference.

After the 1946 biennial, Zionism no longer vexed the Reform movement. Eisendrath could now devote more time and energy to winning the unaffiliated, establishing new congregations, building up the regions, reaching out to Jewish youth, promoting interfaith dialogue, and initiating social justice programs.

His success in steering the Union through three turbulent years of divisiveness enhanced Eisendrath's stature, enabling him to press for a change of title from director to president of the UAHC. He achieved his goal on December 8, 1946, when he was elected president on the very day of Adolph Rosenberg's funeral. Jacob Aronson was named chairman of the executive board.

At that same meeting the board endorsed Eisendrath's controversial proposal to relocate the national headquarters from Cincinnati to New York City. From the time of this endorsement until its ratification at the 1948 Boston biennial, there was, in Jane Evans's words, a "battle royal" over the proposed move.

An article in the UAHC's *Liberal Judaism* listed the principal arguments for relocation to New York:

New York is the organizational center of American and World Jewry; many Christian denominations . . . have their headquarters in New York City; New York is home to the largest Jewish community both in America and the world; and New York is the supreme focal point of contact with the constituent members of the Union. [8]

Opponents of the move insisted that the Union should forever be located in the birthplace of American Reform Judaism. Some declared that Cincinnati, unlike New York, breathed the spirit of America's grass roots, and therefore was more suitable for a lay organization.

At issue was whether the Union would be controlled by a small number of wealthy Cincinnati German Jews who wanted to maintain the status quo or whether its leadership could reach out to the second generation descendants of East European Jewry who had been untouched by the Reform movement. Eisendrath reduced the influence of the Cincinnati faction by increasing the size of the executive board with representation that reflected more accurately the concerns of the Union's regions. A constitutional amendment stipulated that more than half of the members of the executive board had to be elected by the regional organizations.

In his "State of the Union" address at the Boston biennial, Eisendrath argued forcefully for the move:

> We have won less than ten percent of American Jewry to our cause. In those areas, West and South, where but 30 percent of the Jews of America reside, we have gathered some 70 percent of them into our fold. On the Eastern Seaboard with its 75 percent of American Jewry, we boast a bare 30 percent. We must end this incongruity which grows largely out of our erstwhile remoteness. Ours is the inescapable responsibility, strategically to station our heaviest artillery on that front line where must be fought the spiritual and moral struggle to enlist in our ranks the whole of American Jewry which, let us not forget, was the aim of our Founder and his faith-filled followers—not for the sake of mere numbers, but because of our indomitable conviction that what is good for us is also good for all American Jewry and for America itself.

The motion carried. Funds raised by the National Federation of Temple Sisterhoods for a new building were matched by Albert Berg of Congregation Emanu-El, New York. After considerable deliberation, a site was chosen at the corner of 65th Street and Fifth Avenue, opposite Congregation Emanu-El. A mansion located on the site was demolished and a seven-story building erected in its place. The new headquarters, designated the Union House of Living Judaism-Berg Memorial, was dedicated and opened in September 1951.

The move to New York symbolized the transitions taking place in the Union. From a dusty collection of cubbyholes in the Merchants Building in Cincinnati, the Union was now proudly housed in its own impressive building overlooking Central Park in midtown Manhattan. Where once the Union's chief staff member had been a man dominated by the executive board, Eisendrath demonstrated his ability to lead the Union into the dynamic mainstream of American Jewish life. The period 1943–1951 was one of struggle and triumph for Maurice Eisendrath. The years ahead would contain more protracted conflicts but with fewer clear-cut solutions.

REVIVAL AND EXPANSION:
1951-1963

In July of 1952 the executive board elected Maurice Eisendrath as Union president for life. The unanimous vote reflected the board's appreciation for his leadership during the difficult years of transition. In announcing the decision, the board chairman, Dr. Samuel Hollander, stated, "Since he became its president in 1943, the Union has experienced an unusual period of growth, adding more than 150 new congregations to our membership rolls. It is the unanimous desire of the board that Rabbi Eisendrath continue his consecrated and zealous devotion to the Union."

In the first ten years of Eisendrath's leadership (1943–1953), the Union grew from approximately 50,000 to well over 150,000 member families, from about 300 congregations to 460. During the same period the Union's dues collections increased from approximately $150,000 to nearly $1,400,000. [1] UAHC affiliates—the National Federations of Temple Sisterhoods, Brotherhoods, and Youth—reported substantial gains as well during the same period. By the end of the 1950s, the Union claimed 585 congregations in North America, with a total membership of over one million.

In the postwar period, Americans became affiliated with churches and synagogues in unprecedented numbers. The Conservative movement increased at approximately the same rate as Reform. Both also experienced a dramatic rise in religious-school enrollment.

Sociologist Nathan Glazer argued in his book *American Judaism* (1957) that Jewish behavior had to be understood in the context of postwar American society. Americans were migrating out of the big cities and into the suburbs. This movement "reflected not only a rising American prosperity, in which Jews shared, but a change in the social structure of American life, in which occupations historically linked to the lower class and lower-class ways of life tended to be replaced by occupations linked to middle-class ways of life." [2] Wanting to appear respectable to their church-going neighbors, the new suburban Jews joined synagogues.

Historian Bernard Martin disagreed with Glazer's analysis. Martin attributed enhanced Jewish involvement to internal dynamics, such as pride in Israel's achievements and the effects of the Holocaust, which prompted a subconscious desire among American Jews to preserve Judaism.

Whether one places greater emphasis upon external or internal factors, the fact remains that postwar prosperity fueled the unprecedented expansion of Jewish institutions. Given these factors, what role did Eisendrath actually play in the Reform boom?

In 1956, Rabbi Jay Kaufman, assistant to the UAHC president and Eisendrath's closest aide, responded to a board member's assertion that the Union's growth was largely the consequence of events uninfluenced by the Union's leader. Kaufman wrote:

There are those who contend that the magnificent accomplishments of the last decade and a half were a consequence of events which made the Union's growth inevitable. From our close position inside its administration, both you and I know this is not true. The epochal events of the last dozen years have played a substantial role . . . but the Union would not have become what it is today in spite of these events, were it not carefully guided.

Maurice steered the Union into the mainstream of Jewish life and prevented it from becoming a small abortive sect when he faced the then violent subject of Reform and Zionism and succeeded in bringing the Union into the American Jewish Conference and into subsequent Israel centered activities until the present day. It would have been easier to have dodged this issue but the consequences would have been grave. The same is true of the move to New York, the daring expenditures for new congregations in the shadow of older and protesting congregations, the emphasis on more emotionalism and ritual in Reform . . . and scores of such instances in which he collected calumny when by silence or compliance he could have won commendation.

Eugene Borowitz credits Eisendrath's success to his having "had . . . an ideology of what Reform Judaism was and should be about." Eisendrath had the ability to identify issues and trends and to project the importance of his concerns to his staff, the laity, and to the public. "He responded to the situation around him with energy," adds Borowitz, "with a certain amount of vision and concern, and a good deal of resolution and determination."

Winning the unaffiliated was one of Eisendrath's chief concerns in the 1950s. Reform Judaism, in his view, provided an antidote to the "general paganization, despiritualization and demoralization of contemporary American life." Increased membership, of course, generated financial support and demonstrated the importance of the UAHC. He railed against established congregations that sought to block the formation of competing suburban congregations. To promote the emergence of new synagogues, the Union instituted a Synagogue Building Loan Fund in 1955. In later years he would utilize circuit-riding rabbis and mobile synagogues for outreach to the unaffiliated. In addition, Eisendrath upgraded the Union's media profile by insisting on wider distribution of publications, increasing exposure on radio and television, and hiring a public-relations director.

Eisendrath was troubled by the wide diversity of practices in Reform temples:

> Hats on, hats off; one day Rosh Hashana and two days also; Ashkenazic pronunciation and Sefardic; Kosher kitchens in so-called Reform social halls and non-Kosher; Bar Mitzvah encouraged and Bar Mitzvah barred; Confirmation at thirteen, fourteen, fifteen and sixteen; social action and no social action—these are but a few of the countless contradictions in Reform or Liberal temples or synagogues.

Eisendrath frequently cited Isaac Mayer Wise's complaint: "Everyone does what is right in his own eyes. Some call this liberty—I call it license." As early as 1948 and throughout the 1950s Eisendrath called for a consensus on Reform principles and practices in America, both to bring internal consistency to the movement and to make it more attractive to outsiders who derided the evident lack of discipline in Reform Judaism.

Though himself not a demonstrably emotional person in public, Eisendrath appealed for a greater infusion of feeling and mystery into Reform Judaism in order to broaden its appeal among Jews with East European roots. He pointed out that newcomers to the movement who brought with them "a nostalgic love for the folkways, the music, the lore, and the language of our heritage" felt repulsed by the cold rationalism of classical Reform Judaism. Fearing the emergence of a new Orthodoxy, many Reform Jews viewed the attempt to establish uniformity as a betrayal of the movement's ideology. Those raised in anti-ritualistic homes and temples resisted the imposition of Jewish rites rooted in what they regarded as the irrational past. Striving to find a balance, Eisendrath warned that rituals should not become a substitute for religion. He asserted that Isaac Mayer Wise did not seek to abolish all Jewish rituals:

> but neither did he permit the poetry of priestly pageantry to eclipse the behest of prophetic purpose. . . . Rigid custom still dare not replace righteous conduct as the rudimentary requirement of Reform, nor can multiplications of forms supplant the magnification of Faith, nor can vehicles and vestitures displace virtue and personal piety.

Eisendrath supported the allocation of funds for the Union's youth and education programs. The Union's Education Department devised textbook series that were widely used in religious schools of all denominations. In addition, the Union pioneered the use of filmstrips in the classroom. As an adjunct to the religious school, it encouraged the formation of youth groups to enhance Jewish identity among the young. The Union also initiated a camp program, and in 1953 Eisendrath announced the purchase of a facility in Oconomowoc, Wisconsin, the first of what would become a nine-camp network.

Eisendrath attempted to define the Union's relationship with the newly created State of Israel. Publicly he expressed a strong pro-Israel position, leading Union-sponsored tours to Israel. Eisendrath, however, criticized David Ben-Gurion's call for the dissolution of the Diaspora, insisting Israel cannot be rebuilt through a repudiation of American Jewry. "You cannot move a community to great action by playing its funeral march," he warned.

Eisendrath opposed Jews who regarded Israel as the focal point of religious commitment, denouncing what he called the "deification" of the state and the Israeli people:

> If we truly search and try our ways and examine that which prompts each one of us to maintain his Jewish identity, to contribute to UJA or Bonds for Israel, or even to join a synagogue, must we not, in the innermost recesses of our being, confess that sometimes, at least, it *is* an ethnic and national chauvinism, a loyalty to the peoplehood of Israel alone, to the statehood of Israel alone, to the body of Israel rather than to its soul or teachings or moral *mitzvos* that motivate our identification?

> I am not disparaging what Israel can teach a Jew, and what its restoration has meant to many, even to most Jews—and sensitive non-Jews too; but I am challenging this superficial denial of the whole destiny of the Jew which affirms that it was God, and faith in God, and fortitude because of God, which gave the Jew in centuries past . . .

[and] the Jew of today . . . similar spiritual courage and moral daring.

Eisendrath firmly believed that it was the Union's destiny to be oriented toward the Diaspora, not Israel. In 1949 he rebuked the national Jewish welfare funds for spending 99 percent of their receipts to save Jews abroad while neglecting the spiritual needs of Jews at home. He also complained that the "great historic [Reform] congregations with their large rosters of unprecedented wealth" provided insufficient funds for the Union to function. In his "State of Our Union" addresses, Eisendrath consistently reminded the council delegates that members of other Jewish groups (and Christian denominations) were giving more generously to fund-raising campaigns than were Union supporters.

Eisendrath felt frustrated in being unable to expand the Union's activities and influence, dissatisfied that most of the Union's regions lacked full-time directors. Most of his key staff members had come from Cincinnati: Jane Evans at the helm of NFTS, Rabbi Jacob Schwarz, director of the Department of Synagogue Activities; Rabbi Samuel Cook, director of Youth Activities; Rabbi Louis Egelson, administrative secretary; and Dr. Emanuel Gamoran, education director. With the exceptions of Jane Evans and Sam Cook, by the end of the 1950s the older staff members had retired and younger staff had been brought in.

Chief in influence was Rabbi Jay Kaufman. He presided over the day-to-day administration of the Union, a task Eisendrath eschewed. Kaufman, Eisendrath's trusted aide, was an ardent Zionist who had married an Israeli. According to Rabbi Erwin Herman, a former Union staff member, "Jay Kaufman led Maurice into Jerusalem." Though Eisendrath was never fully comfortable with Zionism or Hebrew and was embarrassed when others spoke to him in Hebrew, Kaufman convinced Eisendrath of the importance of Hebrew and Zionism in Reform Jewish education.

In 1951, Rabbi Eugene Lipman joined the staff as the assistant director of the Department of Synagogue Activities, and a year later he succeeded Jacob Schwarz as the full-time director. Lipman, who promoted the creation of new congregations across the country and provided established congregations with program resources, also served as co-director of the National Joint Social Action Commission. The other co-director was Albert Vorspan, whom Eisendrath had wrested from the National Community Relations Advisory Council (NCRAC). Albert Vorspan would become Eisendrath's key advisor in the social action domain.

The coordinating staff of the Union was completed in 1957, when Rabbi Eugene Borowitz joined the Department of Education and Rabbi Erwin Herman came aboard as Rabbi Samuel Cook's assistant at NFTY. Borowitz soon succeeded Gamoran in education, and Herman became national coordinator of the Union's regions.

The willingness of rabbis to join the Union staff indicated a change in the Union's image. As Borowitz put it:

What rabbi ever thought of serving on the Union staff? That's no job for a Jewish boy! . . . When you were a rabbi in the community you were somebody in those days. . . . The hope was you too might be Abba Hillel Silver.

Part of Eisendrath's organizational "genius," according to Borowitz, was that he "sought out ambitious, energetic young men and pretty well turned them loose."

A great deal of improvising took place at the Union in those years. Programs did not unfold according to a set plan; instead, Eisendrath gave his staff free rein to try out their ideas. Some worked, others did not, but a sense of esprit de corps dominated the Union, which viewed itself in the vanguard of Jewish programming.

Eisendrath presided over a managed democracy. Members of the coordinating staff enjoyed easy access to their president, who listened attentively to their concerns. He loved to thrash out an issue in a small group setting, relishing debate and argumentation. Though these small group discussions could become heated, Eisendrath did not take disagreements personally, distinguishing between personal and work relations.

Having no children of his own, he formed paternalistic attachments to certain staff members, particularly to Jay Kaufman and Gene Borowitz.

Eisendrath seemed a reserved and imposing figure to outsiders. In most social situations Eisendrath often felt ill at ease, appearing humorless and awkward. He hardly drank, was a terrible storyteller, and was discomfited when someone told an off-color joke. However, those close to him regarded him differently. Ruth Buchbinder, his secretary for many years, enjoyed her boss's "marvelous sense of humor." [3] At staff parties he would join in the laughter when needled about his inclination to make long speeches, despite his avowal that "brevity is the soul of wit." [4]

Both Maurice and Rosa enjoyed the solitude of their rustic estate in a secluded area of Westchester, New York. Most every summer they returned to a tiny island they had purchased in northern Ontario. For six weeks they would live in a cabin without a phone or running water. Eisendrath's only contact with the Union was a weekly phone call to Jay Kaufman. On the island, Eisendrath could read, think, prepare his addresses, and plan his future course. His excursions into solitude with Rosa followed a prescription articulated during his student years at HUC:

> The religious leader . . . must retire to that ivory tower of solitude, beyond the painful coarseness and desolating barrenness of noisy and confused cities, that through the perspective of distance he might weigh the world objectively, rationally, dispassionately. . . . Out of the darkness which enshrouds us we must formulate . . . a language, out of the black depths, each of us must compose a melody, sweet and ravishing, that the raucous cacophony of our time be transmuted into symphonic poems, into extravagant, rhapsodic diapasons.

As UAHC president, Eisendrath received numerous honors, among them an honorary LL.D. from the University of Cincinnati, Clergyman of the Year (1959) by the Religious Heritage of America, [5] and the first spiritual Freedom Citation from the Chapel of the Four Chaplains. These awards were a source of satisfaction and pride to Eisendrath and gave honor to the UAHC, but one coveted distinction eluded him. He had not become the undisputed spokesman for American Reform Judaism. As long as Nelson Glueck headed the Hebrew Union College, Eisendrath was unable to achieve absolute supremacy within the movement.

The two men held radically different views of the relationship between the Union and the College-Institute (in 1950 the Jewish Institute of Religion in New York merged with HUC). In the words of Professor Michael Meyer:

> Unlike his predecessors, Glueck did not conceive the College to be a ward of the Union; unlike those who came before him, Eisendrath did not see the principal role of the Union to be support of the College. Each believed his own institution should possess primary influence. Eisendrath was of the opinion that the Union, representing the collective will of Reform Jewry through its biennial assemblies, was the fundamental organization of the movement, and as such should control all its national activities, including its centers for the training of rabbis . . . . Glueck, on the other hand, regarded the College-Institute as an autonomous academic institution with only the loosest ties to the UAHC . . . . Eisendrath and Glueck, both capable and ambitious men, were each intent on zealously guarding their institution's prerogatives and on seeking to extend its influence—if necessary at the expense of the other. [6]

Eisendrath and Glueck often clashed over funding. Most of the College-Institute's funds derived from dues paid to the Union by member congregations (called MUM, for Maintenance of Union Membership), and from yearly contributions to the combined Union-College campaign. To achieve his goal of expanding the facilities and influence of his institution, Glueck demanded a greater share of the revenues. By threatening to conduct a separate campaign, Glueck eventually succeeded in winning for the College-Institute half of the receipts of the combined campaign. Eisendrath, of course, resented the depletion of the Union's coffers.

Eisendrath and Glueck also waged a bitter struggle over control of the California College of Jewish Studies. In 1947 the Union established a school in Los Angeles for teacher-training and adult education. A year later, HUC-JIR attached its name to the school, giving it academic credibility, but the Union continued to provide most of the funds. In 1953, Rabbi Isaiah Zeldin was named to direct the UAHC's western region and to serve as dean of the Los Angeles school. In 1957, when the California school sought accreditation, tensions between Glueck and Eisendrath over control of the school intensified. Caught in the middle, Zeldin witnessed one of the skirmishes between the two Reform presidents:

Eisendrath to Glueck: "Where were you all those years that I invested all that money in the College?"

Glueck to Eisendrath: "Well, how much did you pay for it?"

Eisendrath mentioned an outlandish figure of hundreds of thousands of dollars.

Glueck: "O.K., I'll pay you back for all of that!"

Eisendrath to Glueck: "If you want to, I don't want to do it!"

The capping incident came in 1958, when Glueck appointed a board for the Los Angeles campus of HUC without consulting Eisendrath or Zeldin. Zeldin resigned and the College of Jewish Studies was split off from the Hebrew Union College. The training of educators remained under Union supervision until 1968, when the California School of Jewish Education was reincorporated into the Los Angeles campus of HUC-JIR.

The Reform rivals also engaged in a dispute involving ownership of the HUC campus in Cincinnati. After failing to take title of the property from the Union, Glueck ended the long-standing custom of having Union officials sign HUC diplomas. Eisendrath responded by giving less exposure to the College-Institute at the Union biennials and in the pages of the Union publication, *American Judaism.*

Eisendrath demanded staff loyalty, especially in matters pertaining to Glueck. Rabbi Solomon Kleinman, a former UAHC regional director, explained that "Maurice loved you if you could nurture a lay leader who either would . . . give big money or become a strong force in the deliberations of the Union vis-à-vis the conflict with the College." Al Vorspan likened the antagonists to "two scorpions in a bottle." Alarmed by the extent of the intramural struggle, CCAR president Rabbi Jacob Rudin declared in his 1958 president's message:

> Reform Judaism cannot afford the instability of uncertain peace nor the luxury of unamiable controversy. This is not a contained, limited struggle. Reform Judaism in America is the casualty. Everybody gets hurt. Every national interest is endangered.

When Glueck gave the benediction at John F. Kennedy's inauguration or appeared on the cover of *Time* magazine in 1963, Eisendrath redoubled his efforts to gain ascendancy as the recognized spokesman for Reform Judaism.

However, a letter to Eisendrath in 1958, prompted by the tragic death of Barnett Brickner in an automobile accident in Spain, reveals that Glueck bore no personal animosity toward the UAHC president:

> Let us count our blessings while we may, my friend. How can we be so foolish as to be angry at one another? I clasp your hands and vow to do everything possible—so inwardly I believe I always have—to work with you for our single cause. There are times when we will not see eye to eye, but let it be regarded as honest difference of judgments and let no one whisper in our ears that it is animosity. Life is difficult and short. The work is great and the cause is enduring and the workers are all too few. And however much we succeed in advancing the work of God entrusted to us, it must inevitably fall far short of what remains to be done. And so I salute you and Rosa with all my heart and pray for your health and well-being and for the blessing of everything we hold dear. Your success is my gain, and your happiness my enduring hope.

Despite their long-standing rivalry, Eisendrath downplayed his conflict with Glueck in an interview conducted in 1972, more than a year after Glueck's death and a year before his own. Eisendrath indicated that it would have been a miracle if two men, heading their respective institutions, had not disagreed. Eisendrath stated their disputes were largely over money and harmoniously resolved:

> I don't think we were enemies. We each respected the other. There were times when I felt that deep inside I was very fond of Nelson Glueck.

It is questionable whether Maurice Eisendrath and Nelson Glueck eventually resolved their differences. Some report that there was animosity between the two up until Glueck's death. Others say that in later years there was a mellowing in their relationship.

Their rivalry was a mixed blessing for the Reform movement. Although Glueck and Eisendrath's bitter struggle for supremacy polarized and demoralized the lay leadership, their intense institutional competition spurred the growth of their respective institutions.

"WITH MORAL INDIGNATION AND RIGHTEOUS PROTEST"

One of Maurice Eisendrath's reasons for choosing to become a rabbi was his simple desire to do good in the world. Raised in a classical Reform tradition, he believed in the ultimate perfectibility of human beings. He believed that the world, though filled with corruption and immorality, could be redeemed if everyone would heed the holy demand to do justice and love mercy. The messianic age would be inaugurated not by a personal messiah but by the righteous actions of each individual. Inspired by the biblical prophets who emphasized the transcendent God of the universe over the particular God of a single people, Eisendrath believed that God demanded action rather than worship, justice rather than obedience. The essence of Judaism, according to classical Reform, was ethics and not the fulfillment of ritual obligations.

Eisendrath held to his youthful idealism, never doubting that ethics formed the core of Judaism. He characterized Israel not as God's chosen people but, in Rabbi Mordecai Kaplan's words, as a "choosing people" confronted with the choice of acting righteously or not.

In a sermon entitled "Retreat or Advance," delivered at the 1937 CCAR convention in Columbus, Ohio, Eisendrath exhorted his colleagues to lead their flocks to the Promised Land:

And great indeed is the temptation to temporize, to ooze sweetness and light, to "salve with pastor oil" the caprices of the congregation, to outshout the aspiring politicians and professional jingoes who seek to hold the mass in the palm of their hands.

Far different must our true rabbinic function be . . . that war is wrong; that human exploitation is wrong; that economic inequity is wrong; that dictatorships of the right or of the left . . . are wrong; that rigid custom, instead of righteous conduct, that a multiplication of form rather than the magnification of faith, is wrong; that to confuse means with ends, husk with kernel, vehicles with virtues, fleshpots with goals and spiritual ideals, is wrong; that retreat rather than advance, that sheep-like following rather than God-like leading is wrong—such must be the burden of our ministry.

In his first statement as the director of the Union, Eisendrath called on the organization to fulfill the mission of Israel:

A comprehensive knowledge of our heritage demands that we make the effort, as did Ezekiel and Deutero-Isaiah, as did the rabbis of our Talmud and the writers of our Midrash, as did a Judah ha-Levi . . . all of whom, despite their zealous particularism, desired to make of Israel a "goy kodosh," "a holy people," nonetheless never lost sight of the particular function of the Jews as a "mamleches kohanim," as a kingdom of priests consecrated to the service of mankind.

And this unique synthesis [of universalism and particularism] of which I speak is not only our own, but the world's most pressing need.

Reform rabbis had for many decades sermonized about the "mission of Israel" to the nations of the world, but Eisendrath infused this Jewish ethical imperative with a sense of immediacy and urgency. At the 1946 Union biennial, he lamented how Jews were content merely to talk about social justice and regretted that the Union had "surrendered" the field of social action to nonreligious agencies such as the American Jewish

Committee. Religious organizations such as the Union, he insisted, not secular agencies, should be undertaking the sacred work of the ancient prophets. Expressing embarrassment that many church groups had social justice and peace committees, he called for the formation of a commission on social action, possibly in conjunction with the CCAR. [1]

Two years later Eisendrath outlined some of the concerns he felt the commission should address.

> With regard to the conflict between labor and management; . . . in the tangled, troubled realm of race relations; in the sordid international game of power politics; in the face of the impending immoral use of atomic power; religion, Judaism, Liberal, prophetic Judaism, must have its say; must speak its mind; point the finger, name the name, and do the righteous deed!

A joint UAHC-CCAR social action commission was organized in 1949 but gained little momentum until 1953, when Joseph McCarthy's Senate hearings provoked a "deepening moral crisis" of the American spirit that Eisendrath determined to combat with an effective social action program. An internal UAHC development added impetus to Eisendrath's decision to upgrade social action. When UAHC employees proposed to unionize, the executive board opposed the move, indicating that a significant gap existed between ideology and practice among the lay leadership.

Eisendrath recruited Albert Vorspan to serve as executive secretary of the UAHC-CCAR Joint Commission on Social Action. This move surprised some people. Vorspan was not a rabbi, yet he had been chosen for a newly created position on the Union staff. The selection of a professional in the area of social action and public relations signified Eisendrath's determination to place social action at the top of the Union's agenda. The commission's purpose would be "to stimulate similar social action committees in every one of our constituent congregations, to provide syllabi for study and action on the local scene, to prepare religious school texts so that our children and youth may have a clearer and more tangible appreciation of the bearing of liberal prophetic Judaism upon the moral, social, economic, political and international problems which everywhere confront and trouble them."

Under the leadership of Vorspan and Eugene Lipman, director, the commission undertook its work with seriousness and energy, expanding to include the NFTB, NFTS, and NFTY in its successful effort to stimulate the formation of social action committees in temples. In 1956 the UAHC published *Justice and Judaism*, a textbook by Vorspan and Lipman that explored the Jewish concept of religious action as it applied to domestic and international issues.

Civil rights for blacks became a key UAHC concern in the mid-1950s, prompted by the Supreme Court's decision on *Brown* v. *Board of Education.* Eisendrath encountered significant congregational resistance to his outspoken pronouncements in support of racial justice, especially in the South. In response to an article in which Eisendrath expressed his support for the Montgomery, Alabama, bus boycott and advocated establishing a UAHC social action committee in the South, Myron J. Rothschild, president of Montgomery's Temple Beth Or, responded:

> I am fully acquainted with the thinking of the vast majority of reformed [*sic*] Jewry in the Southeast and as such I do not hesitate to say to you that we do not wish an office of the Social Action Committee established in the South. We do not need it. Our thinking is so entirely different from yours, that we have come to the conclusion that we really do not need your advice. I will be charitable in my thinking and say that we think you simply do not understand the problems of the South.

He accused Eisendrath of endangering the welfare of all Southern congregations by potentially stirring up a "tremendous wave of anti-Semitism." Rothschild sent a copy of his letter to members of the Union's executive board.

Eisendrath rejected Rothschild's presumption to speak for the South as a whole. Conceding that he did not know the South as well as some, Eisendrath wrote, "One did not have to

live in Nazi Germany to be certain that our brethren were bes-
tially butchered." The Union president expressed dismay that
people like Rothschild refused to acknowledge the problem.
Rather than feeling "chagrin and shame and a deep sense of
both personal and corporate guilt concerning the existence of
prejudice and bigotry, exclusion and segregation," he wrote, too
many felt "smug self-righteousness." Eisendrath added that
Southern Jews should be prepared to make sacrifices in
defense of principles:

> Our fathers sought no such "good will" at any price but
> rather pursued God's will at any cost, certainly of economic
> loss, ostracism, exile, and even death. If surrender to major-
> ity opinion had been the standard of Jewish practice, then
> we would not be discussing this matter as Jews today.

He concluded with the wish that he and Rothschild reach
some "common understanding in brotherly forbearance."

Two years later, in 1958, the Board of Trustees (the new
title for the executive board) of the Union passed a resolution
commending the brave actions of many Southern rabbis and
congregations in the struggle for human equality in their area.
Eisendrath, however, felt that neither the Southern nor
Northern Jews had gone far enough in combatting racial dis-
crimination.

The UAHC's 45th General Assembly was scheduled to meet
in the South, in Miami, in November of 1959. Eisendrath
wanted to invite Dr. Martin Luther King, whom he likened to
"the Gandhi of our nation and of our generation." Eisendrath,
however, had to withdraw the invitation as a result of strong
internal opposition. Frustrated and angry, he did not heed the
advice to tone his Union address. Eisendrath unleashed his
wrath upon his people's shortcomings:

> And with regard to the . . . desideratum, which whispers to
> my sense of propriety, of *derech eretz* to avoid this theme
> [civil rights] . . . because of our convening for the first time
> in this center contiguous to the deep South, I could not
> evade the stinging reminder that the sin of segregation—*sin
> it is*—is the monopoly of no region, for brotherhood is indi-

visible. What I have in mind, as I plunge once more into this heinous transgression of God's Fatherhood and man's all inclusive brotherhood is the whole vast miasma of venomous racial hatred and segregation which rises like a stink in God's nostrils.

In later years, Eisendrath marched with Dr. King and repeatedly urged the Union to pass resolutions which expressed its commitment to racial justice. Even in the mid- and late-1960s, when Jews reacted with frustration and pain to the rejection by some black leaders, Eisendrath continued to seek to ameliorate the conditions of black people. Addressing the UAHC board in 1966, he stated:

> Regrettably some of these charges [of black militancy and anti-Semitism] are at least partially true. . . . Nor can we condone such conduct which has characterized some segments of the Negro community. We cannot condone irrational antagonism, indiscriminate name-calling, irresponsible sloganeering, hoodlumism, or wanton violence. . . . [Yet] Jews—who, not as any quid pro quo, but as an absolute, unequivocal mandate, are bidden to "love our neighbor as ourself" whether or not that neighbor requites our love and whether or not that neighbor may conceivably have caught the disease of anti-Semitism from his white milieu.

Three years later he expressed support for the payment of reparations to black Americans: "Call it reparations or simple justice, but some form of restitution we do owe to those whose blood and enslavement in menial jobs and incarceration in stinking, fetid, rat-infested slums [contributed to] our own prosperity." He continued to address the issue of civil rights long after many Jews had turned their attention to more particular Jewish concerns.

From 1959 to 1962 Eisendrath devoted much of his energy to winning support for the creation of a national Reform center for religious action in Washington, D.C. Prior to the 1959 biennial, Emily and Kivie Kaplan had pledged $100,000 toward this end. Eisendrath and the majority of the board members

favored creating the center, which would serve as a branch of
the Joint Commission on Social Action, disseminating informa-
tion about the Union's position on issues and sponsoring educational seminars.

Despite strong opposition, delegates to the 1959 biennial
approved the creation of the Religious Action Center and, a
year later, the Union purchased a building on Massachusetts
Avenue, N.W. Five congregations, the most prominent of
which were the Washington Hebrew Congregation and
Congregation Emanu-El of New York, passed resolutions condemning the Religious Action Center. An article by Ben
Firestone in *Congress Bi-Weekly* summarized their concerns:

> Some were vehemently opposed to social action altogether,
> holding that the application of Jewish ethics to social issues
> and daily life was the duty of the individual and not of the
> synagogue or of the Reform Jewish movement. Some were
> strongly opposed to the idea of a social action center in
> Washington, fearing it would smack of "lobbying" and would
> involve Reform synagogues in "controversial" issues. Some
> Southerners objected because of UAHC positions on deseg-
> regation. The American Council for Judaism loosed a wild
> charge that the Center was part of some dark trend toward
> "monolithic" institutions. One or two others, unconcerned
> with social action one way or the other, saw in the issue an
> opportunity to challenge the leadership and basic direction
> of the UAHC. [2]

In response, the UAHC leadership decided to open the issue
for reconsideration at the next General Assembly. Prior to the
biennial, to be held in Washington, D.C., the Washington
Hebrew Congregation distributed its "Statement of Principle
for Reform Jewish Congregations," asserting that the Union
did not represent Reform Jews on legislative, economic, political, and social issues. The Washington congregation rejected
the notion of a "Reform Jewish viewpoint or even a Jewish
viewpoint," maintaining that "backgrounds, experience, and
beliefs lead Reform Jews to take many different positions on
social, economic, and political questions." The Union, they
insisted, should limit its activities in the area of social action to
study and research.

In defense of the Religious Action Center, the Union published and distributed a pamphlet entitled "Twenty Questions on Reform Judaism and Social Action." The anonymous author conceded that every congregation in the Union had the right to protest a decision by the General Assembly. According to the Union's constitution, no congregation was bound by UAHC statements or decisions. Nevertheless, a mandate for the establishment of the RAC had been given at the 1959 biennial, proving that the majority wanted Reform Jewry to raise its profile in the nation's capital.

At the 1961 biennial, opponents of the RAC sought to limit the scope of the center's operation rather than to oppose social action altogether. Their strategy failed. According to an eyewitness:

> Even in the early stages of the debate it became evident where the sentiments of the delegates lay. The opposition to the Center was singularly unpersuasive. The vote was overwhelming—approximately 1,200 to 100. A triumphant roar of gratification echoed through the hall, almost drowning out the chairman's announcement that the amendments were defeated and the main resolution carried.[3]

At the dedication of the Religious Action Center on November 30, 1962, Eisendrath expressed satisfaction that after "a bitter, costly struggle" social action had prevailed.

In 1965 Eisendrath spoke out against the Vietnam War, one of the few Jewish leaders daring to do so. Although he had abandoned pacifism during the Holocaust years, Eisendrath viewed religion in general, and Judaism in particular, as a means to build bridges of peace between nationalities in conflict. In 1957 he had embarked on a five-month world tour, meeting religious and political leaders to discuss ways of achieving world peace. His itinerary included talks with Prime Minister Nehru of India, Prince Mikasa of Japan, General Chiang Kai-shek of Nationalist China, and Prime Minister Menzies of Australia.

In 1966 Eisendrath convened and co-chaired the first National Inter-Religious Conference on Peace, and in 1970 he helped organize the first International Conference on Religion and Peace, convened in Kyoto, Japan.

Eisendrath pursued world peace with a sense of urgency, recognizing that the advent of nuclear weapons placed the entire world at risk. In 1950 he offered a morose analysis of the conflict in Korea: "The cold war which is now so speedily catapulting all of us into the hot war, which we have so tremblingly feared will this time be no comparatively harmless 'kinderspiel' of rifles and bayonets, cannons and tanks . . . but will unfold the more adult pastimes of nation hurling atom bomb at nation until by mutual self-destruction and world annihilation 'they learn war no more.'" In a report to the Board of Trustees in 1959, Eisendrath warned:

> We must awaken from our seeming stupor and our selfish immersion in pleasure and profit to take more seriously the warnings of an increasing number of scientists concerning the terrifying race toward world suicide. . . . We must . . . transcend narrow national self-interest in seeking, even at the price of certain risks and sacrifices, to remove from our time the harrowing threat of world incineration.

Eisendrath opposed nuclear testing unequivocally and appealed for total nuclear disarmament.

The year 1965 marked an escalation of the United States's involvement in Vietnam. In his report to the Board of Trustees in May of that year, following President Lyndon Johnson's reinforcing of U.S. troops, Eisendrath condemned the American attempt to "stroll the world like 'a star-studded Texas sheriff' to impose *our* brand of law and order upon the entire world." He supported a resolution calling for a negotiated settlement to the conflict. Six months later he made Vietnam a subject of his address to the Union's General Assembly. He cited the Pope's U.N. plea for peace and a *New York Times* editorial, affirming the right of every American to dissent from the government's policies.

Eisendrath sensed he was in the minority on this issue, even among Reform Jews. Most Americans accepted the government's statements that U.S. combat troops were necessary to assist South Vietnam in defending its territory from Communist aggression. Only a few other Jewish leaders, notably Rabbi Jacob Weinstein, president of the CCAR, Rabbi Abraham Joshua Heschel of the Jewish Theological Seminary, and Rabbi Roland Gittelsohn of Temple Israel, Boston, openly opposed the war. [4]

At the 1965 UAHC biennial a resolution was passed calling for a ceasefire in Vietnam and for negotiations between the hostile parties. These demands were highly controversial and were buried in a more generally worded resolution about achieving world peace.

Eisendrath condemned the war, not only because it brought violence and destruction to the Vietnamese people, but because it diverted precious resources from the war against poverty in America. In response to the race riots of summer 1967, he declared, "There is an epitaph which will haunt us long after we escape the mire in Vietnam: 'Here lies the American city, doomed to decay and despair, a tinderbox for violence and insurrection.'"

At the 1967 UAHC biennial, Eisendrath stated:

As more and more of our young men are drafted and torn to bits in the maw of Mars, as more and yet more "bombs bursting in air" sear the flesh, sometimes of cunning, cruel and sadistic adversaries it is true, but perhaps even more frequently of innocent men, women, and children in their rice paddies and villages . . . we ought to split the sky with moral indignation and righteous protest.

Through most of the mid- to late-1960s, the organized American Jewish community was divided on Vietnam. Despite opposition, Eisendrath consistently voiced his outrage and condemnation of the war. Congregation Emanu-El of New York responded to Eisendrath's public antiwar stance by withdrawing from the Union. The congregation's board accused Eisendrath of voicing "unauthorized and impossible" statements about the war while purporting to speak for the entire Reform movement. Emanu-El found particularly "offensive" Eisendrath's open letter to President Johnson in the Winter

1967 issue of *American Judaism*. Eisendrath had protested
Johnson's refusal to meet with religious leaders whose views of
the war differed from those of the White House. He also had
criticized Johnson's alleged attempt to silence the Jewish community by threatening to cut foreign aid to Israel. Emanu-El's
board took particular offense at Eisendrath's veiled comparison
of Johnson to the ancient Syrian tyrant, Antiochus:

> If he [Antiochus] wanted to wage a war, no matter how
> small and weak the opponent might be or how superior his
> destructive weapons, he demanded one hundred per cent
> consensus. . . . But those stubborn mulish Jews refused. . . .
> Rallying to the heroic challenge of a few of the troublesome
> Jewish leaders, they revolted and defeated the conformity-
> craving Antiochus.

The Union president later issued an apology for the article
to his own board. According to a *New York Times* article dated
May 30, 1967, he reportedly said that as an "emotional and
zealous person he sometimes said or wrote things in the heat
of the moment he might wish to erase later." Nonetheless,
Eisendrath railed against Congregation Emanu-El for seceding
from the Union.

Congregation Emanu-El's withdrawal did little to dissuade
Eisendrath from continuing to voice his opposition to the war.
In 1969 he endorsed, along with other prominent antiwar
activists, a one-day moratorium on Vietnam to be held October
15. Later, he berated the Nixon administration, charging that
while Nixon pledged to draw all Americans together, he
encouraged his vice president, Spiro Agnew, and others to
"drive them wrathfully apart." He warned in the *Cincinnati
Enquirer* that the administration was injecting the American
public with "carefully calibrated viruses of hate."

As much as Eisendrath was an outspoken critic of the government's conduct of the war, he never called for a fundamental change in the American political system. As a liberal
whose politics were grounded in the Judaic quest for justice
and peace, he viewed the war in Vietnam and the struggle for
civil rights as moral crises of the American spirit.

Eisendrath fulfilled the prophet's task of awakening the people to their errors. A reaffirmation of traditional values, rather than a revolutionary call for a new society, motivated him. Some questioned his sincerity in regard to his stands on social action. He avoided situations that might result in his arrest and incarceration. His pronouncements were viewed by his detractors as publicity-seeking. One interviewee recalled with displeasure Eisendrath's eagerness to be photographed with Martin Luther King, Jr., as if this confirmed the Union president's stature in the civil rights movement.

Eisendrath himself faulted his unwillingness to assume personal risk. In a report to the board in May 1967 he stated, "I feel not pride but chagrin that I have said so little, my deeds have been so puny. I have not prophetically pioneered, but I have gingerly followed the lead of others. I have been neither as radical or revolutionary as these times demand. I have never stood alone as my understanding of Judaism and my conscience should have demanded." He concluded his remarks with an expression of admiration for Abraham Joshua Heschel, whom Eisendrath regarded as a true prophet.

Yet something more than a desire to be in the public eye prompted Eisendrath to hammer away at issues of conscience. He faced considerable opposition to his stands, both in and out of the UAHC, but his strong sense of inner conviction enabled him to prevail. Rabbi Joseph Glaser, former director of the Union's Northern California region, remembered the first biennial he attended. It was in Miami in 1959. Eisendrath had already given an hour-long "State of Our Union" address which "took a hell of a lot out of him." He had also met with the board. Nonetheless, he called for a midnight staff meeting:

"He came in looking fresh as a daisy and said, 'We must organize to pass a resolution on nuclear disarmament.'

"I was amazed. I had expected some kind of in-house matter such as dues to be paid by congregations to the Union. But his concern was quite elsewhere that night. That's when I knew he was for real. A man of principle, courage, and social conscience; someone really in the prophetic tradition."

In the 1950s and 1960s, social activism became a litmus test of Reform Jewish identity. Yet two events prompted a reexamination of the Reform Jewish commitment to social action. Some blacks rejected Jewish participation in the civil rights movement, leaving many Jews feeling betrayed and hurt. In addition, Israel's isolation prior to June 1967, and its subsequent victory in the Six-Day War, provoked many Diaspora Jews to abandon universal causes in favor of all-out support for the Jewish state. Though the times were changing, Eisendrath was too set in his ways to adapt suitably, too identified with the cause of social action. By the late 1960s he became increasingly isolated as a leader of Reform Jewry.

Maurice Eisendrath, left, with brother, Arthur, and sister, Juliette.
Courtesy of the American Jewish Archives, HUC-JIR, Cincinnati.

1926 ordination, Hebrew Union College. Eisendrath is standing, second from left. Courtesy of the author.

Eisendrath as rabbi of Holy Blossom Temple, Toronto, Canada, c. 1930.
Courtesy of the American Jewish Archives, HUC-JIR, Cincinnati.

With Israeli Prime Minister David Ben-Gurion, 1953.
To Eisendrath's left is his wife Rosa and Rabbi Herman Schaalman.
Courtesy of the American Jewish Archives, HUC-JIR, Cincinnati.

Maurice and Rosa Eisendrath celebrating his thirteenth anniversary as UAHC president, 1956.
Courtesy of the author.

Eisendrath on vacation at his country home on the island of Tamagami, Canada.
Courtesy of the American Jewish Archives, HUC-JIR, Cincinnati.

Eisendrath presents Torah to President John F. Kennedy, left, at the White House, 1963. At his right are Supreme Court Justice Arthur Goldberg and Judge Emil Baar, chairman of the UAHC Board of Trustees. Courtesy of the UAHC.

Maurice and Rita Eisendrath with UAHC Regional Director
Rabbi Morris Hershman and his wife Geraldine, 1973.
Courtesy of the author.

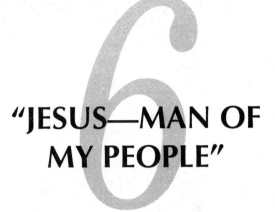

"JESUS—MAN OF MY PEOPLE"

Promoting Jewish-Christian understanding was a primary concern of Maurice Eisendrath throughout his years in the rabbinate. He decried "hypocritical cookie-pushing, back-slapping interfaith teas and sham interreligious dinners . . . that face no realities and build no substantial bridges." He believed that united social action was the key to interfaith relations. In Canada, the United States, and even internationally, Eisendrath had successfully built bridges to other faiths on the basis of mutual concern about social issues.

But he encountered considerable opposition among his own people when he spoke theologically about interfaith relations. In Chicago on November 16, 1963, Maurice Eisendrath delivered his customary "State of Our Union" address to the General Assembly. He spoke at length about the accomplishments of the Reform movement and the challenges it faced in the years ahead. Eisendrath then focused his remarks on relations between Christians and Jews, responding to news that the Catholic Church might revise its official doctrine regarding Jewish culpability in the crucifixion:

> The mind is staggered and the heart is enkindled simply by the prospect of the possible implications of the Catholic Church's official disassociation from the age-old charge of deicide leveled against the Jewish people. . . . This could

have so enormous an effect on Jewish life here and throughout the world as to lead not only to a repudiation of anti-
Semitism but also to a positive Christian thrust against it.

In typical bold fashion, Eisendrath called upon his fellow
Jews to evaluate their own statements and interpretations of
the significance of the life of Jesus, asking rhetorically, "Have
we examined our own books, official and otherwise, to reappraise our ofttimes jaundiced view of him in whose name
Christianity was established?" Eisendrath went on to charac-
terize Jesus as a Jew who offered a lofty yet simply stated message that was thoroughly grounded in prophetic and rabbinic
thought. "How long would it be," he queried, "until Jews would
reclaim Jesus as one of their own and admit that Jesus' influ-
encc was beneficial, not only to pagans, but to the Jew of his
time as well, and that only those who later took his name in
vain profaned his teaching?"

Reactions to Eisendrath's appeal were swift and heated.
While some rabbis quietly expressed their support of his views,
those who vehemently opposed him attracted wide press cover-
age. *Time* magazine quoted Nelson Glueck's view that
Eisendrath's statement made it seem "as if American Reform
Judaism was prepared to put Jesus in a central role as a great
rabbinical leader."[1] Having just opened a branch of the HUC-
JIR in Jerusalem, Glueck was concerned that Eisendrath's
remarks "would set back the progress of Liberal Judaism in
Israel for forty or fifty years."

Rabbi Norman Lamm, writing in the *Rabbinical Council
Record*, had Eisendrath in mind when he castigated a Reform
leader for overreacting to the proposed changes in Church doctrine. This Reform leader's elation and gratitude, he said, rep-
resented an utter abandonment of sensible judgment. "Only a
subservient obsequious, negative personality who has no self-
respect will thank his tormentors for calling off his playful tor-
tures."[2]

An editorial in the *Congress Bi-weekly* excoriated
Eisendrath for linking his remarks about Jesus to the
Ecumenical Council in Rome. The editorial said that the

council's proposed removal of the charge of deicide against the Jews would be an act of historic justice, which should elicit from Jews deep satisfaction. However, an exaggerated show of gratitude was unseemly. Furthermore, the council's proposed action did not obligate the Jewish community to respond quid pro quo. The editorial concluded:

> It is highly dubious whether the Christian world, which is concerned with the divinity of Jesus, will look with special favor upon Jews for elevating Jesus to the rank of a Jewish prophet. As for Jews, their pantheon of prophets is already crowded. [3]

Some offered more tempered criticisms. Rabbi Leonard Winograd complained that Eisendrath's view would encourage intermarriage and assimilation. [4] Rabbi Balfour Brickner, a member of the Union's staff, was quoted in *Newsweek* as saying that "Jews are just as suspicious of Christian theology as they have always been. No attempt should be made now to equate the Roman Catholic ecumenical spirit and reforms within Judaism." [5]

Eisendrath refused to retract a single word of his controversial pronouncements before the Union's General Assembly. In the December 2, 1963, issue of *Newsweek*, he stated that his remarks were a response both to the Vatican and to the times:

> I do firmly believe a new mood is welling up in the world. My thought is just to remove those areas of discord and irritation that can be removed.

In a chapter of his book *Can Faith Survive?*, entitled "Jesus—Man of My People," Eisendrath expressed dismay about the absence of a tolerant response to study the relationship of Judaism and Jesus objectively. His "harmless appeal" was "greeted with an almost visceral and vehement rejection— not so much by laymen, but by many rabbis to whom the very mention of the name of Jesus is forbidden." Eisendrath recognized that Jews have long suffered at the hands of Christians and had good reason to distrust the Church. Nevertheless, he called upon Jews to draw a sharp line between the religion *of* Jesus and the religion *about* Jesus. Eisendrath believed that

Jesus was a historical personality, born in the Galilee, reared as a Pharisee, and influenced by John the Baptist. A wandering teacher, he was hailed as the messiah, then seized and executed by command of Pontius Pilate. It was Paul who created the religion called Christianity. Paul conceived of Jesus as the Son of God and declared that salvation came only through belief in Jesus. The Gospels' hostile portrayal of Jews reinforced the Christians in the struggles between Judaism and the nascent Christian Church.

Eisendrath argued that Jesus was not an apostate but a loyal and devoted son of Israel. This conclusion, he claimed, was "the irrefutable finding of contemporary Biblical science." He cited a number of Christian scholars, such as Julius Wellhausen, George Foot Moore, Shirley Jackson Case, and James Parkes, whose writings substantiated his own viewpoint. He also quoted a number of notable Reform Jewish leaders such as Isaac Mayer Wise, Stephen S. Wise, Leo Baeck, Solomon Freehof, and even Nelson Glueck, all of whom had made approving comments about Jesus.

In Eisendrath's view, the religion of Jesus was pure and unadulterated Judaism. Jesus was beloved by the Jewish people of his time. He was "one of the noblest, most loyal and faithful Jews who ever lived, a Jew who combined in his majestic personality 'all that was best and most enchanting in Israel—the eternal people whose child he was.'"

Eisendrath believed that Jewish life could be richly enhanced by his restoration to a proper place among Jewish teachers and sages. Parables about Jesus could be included among stories of Moses and Hillel. Even the Sermon on the Mount could be read in the synagogue.

Eisendrath neglected to acknowledge that he selectively incorporated the views of some Reform Jewish leaders while ignoring those of others. [6] Dr. Julian Morgenstern, for example, had published an article in the *American Israelite* (1905) condemning Jews who adulated Jesus as a great teacher and reformer:

"It is painful to hear the same gush and twaddle year after

year arising partly out of ignorance and lack of historical discriminative ability and partly out of our sycophantic desire to appease the religious scruples of our Christian brothers irritated by our denial of the god-head of Jesus."

In 1941 Rabbi Max Raisin bitterly attacked Reform Jews who acclaimed Jesus as a Jewish prophet and teacher, warning that any Reform Jewish leader who spoke approvingly of Jesus would weaken Judaism and provide the impetus for assimilation and conversion. Raisin argued that Jesus no longer belonged to the Jews: "He had been stolen from us and the theft is irrecoverable."

Eisendrath's own view of Jesus had undergone certain changes, although he always maintained that Jesus was born and reared, lived and died, as a Jew. In December, Eisendrath, as a congregational rabbi, customarily gave a sermon about Jesus, Christianity, and Judaism. In 1928 Eisendrath stated that certain Jews may have been implicated in Jesus' arrest:

Maybe some Jews were instrumental in betraying him, maybe a few aristocrats in Jewry found his teachings imprudent and unsafe, maybe some of the more powerful deemed his doctrines radical, dangerous and bolshevistic. Perhaps they did join the rabble who turned this troublemaker in Israel, this conscientious Jewish objector over to the authorities in Israel.

Nine years later, when the situation of Jews in Europe had worsened considerably, he gave a very different interpretation of the events that transpired before Jesus' death. Aware that Nazis were utilizing the Gospel of John as justification for persecuting Jews, Eisendrath sought to exonerate all Jews of any connection with the crucifixion. Eisendrath portrayed Jesus as a political agitator who threatened the Roman authorities. If indeed Jesus had made a so-called triumphal entry into Jerusalem, the Romans had their justification for the arrest and execution of Jesus.

Eisendrath later revised his portrait of Jesus as a rebel and a troublemaker; rather, he spoke of the similarities between Jesus and Reform Judaism. Both Jesus and Reform Judaism followed the prophetic tradition of emphasizing the inner principles of Judaism over superficial displays of religiosity.

Eisendrath spoke about Jesus because he wished to move beyond the centuries-old animosities between the two faiths. The European Enlightenment and the freedom enjoyed by Jews in the United States prompted Jews like Eisendrath to reappraise Jesus and Christianity. Professor Samuel Sandmel's remarks about Isaac Mayer Wise's attitude toward Jesus apply also to Eisendrath:

"The age of antipathy . . . was inconsistent with an age of enlightenment and broad horizons. . . . There was no spiritual or physical ghetto in the United States, and Jews and Christians lived side by side in a relatively high state of harmony and good will. Christianity inevitably intruded into the consciousness of Jews and so did Jesus.

"[Wise] was moved to write because no Jew breathing the free air of America could refrain from coming to grips in some way with Christianity and with Jesus . . . . Wise wrote because he had to write; he could not be a leader of an American Jewish community and not do so." [7]

Eisendrath, however, underestimated the latent tension in Jewish-Christian relations. It may be because Eisendrath was American born and had not personally encountered intense anti-Semitism that he never seriously questioned a tenet of nineteenth-century Reform Judaism—that the Jew was the moral leavening in the greater society whose duty it was to promote harmony among all people. He was painfully aware of the history of sufferings Jews had experienced at the hands of Christians, but not even the Holocaust affected his optimistic view of the role of the Jew in the world. In fact he had some harsh words for those Jews who did not support the cause of universal brotherhood. In a pamphlet entitled *A Jewish Platform of Good Will*, published by the National Conference of Christians and Jews, he wrote:

"Even to this day [1953] there are undoubtedly some who, smarting at the memory of centuries of nightmarish incarceration in ghettos, and more recently in barbed wire concentration camps, fight shy of movements of good will and remain aloof from such desirable efforts to build human brotherhood as the National Conference of Christians and Jews. For some of these the vivid recollection of pogrom and yellow badge, of ritual murder and mass cremations, may seem still too recent to permit them to 'love *all* one's neighbors as one's self.'

"These few are not true to their Torah, are not obedient to the Jewish Moral Law. Though their motivation may be understood, though a sympathetic sensitive understanding of the valley of the shadow through which their people and sometimes their very selves have passed cannot be overlooked, nevertheless their heritage as Jews precludes any such seclusive reaction."

It is doubtful whether many Jews living in 1953 or 1963 could devalue the devastating effects of the Holocaust or the sufferings that preceded it. The hostile response to Eisendrath's remarks at the Chicago biennial indicated that for many Jews, Jesus was not an idealized Reform Jew or Jewish prophet or Jewish teacher. Jesus was the symbol, par excellence, of Christianity and the potential fury non-Jews could direct at Jews. Eisendrath never comprehended this viewpoint.

More than with any other proposal he placed before the General Assembly, on the subject of Jesus Eisendrath was unable to inspire his listeners to change their views. This failure never seriously affected his standing within the Reform movement. It is noteworthy that as a social activist, Eisendrath was very successful in motivating others to take progressive stands on issues such as racial justice, Vietnam, and nuclear war. But when he called for Jews to reevaluate the relation of Jesus to Judaism, he did not succeed. He failed because of his inadequate conception of Jesus and because on this issue he did not understand fully the feelings of American Jews.

SLOWED STEPS: 1963-1973

By the mid-1960s, Maurice Eisendrath had reached a pinnacle in his career as president of the UAHC. He had shaped the Union into an effective organization, providing direction and resources in the fields of education, worship, synagogue administration, and social justice. He was recognized as a major spokesman for a movement of nearly one million American Jews. Eisendrath's public persona was well known. Less understood was the private man, the focus of this chapter.

During their five-month global tour for peace in 1958, Rosa fell ill in India. She may have been suffering from the first signs of the disease that eventually caused her death. Though Rosa was a woman of uncommon courage, she once said to Maurice, "If I ever have it [cancer], I don't want to know." [1] Eisendrath honored her request. During the final weeks of Rosa's life, he remained at her side, leaving the daily decisions of the Union to his staff.

Rosa died on July 2, 1963. In a memorial tribute, Albert Vorspan praised her as a woman who gladly abandoned a promising musical career in order to be a helpmate to her husband. Despite her own considerable achievements in communal life—she had been active in the World Council of Women, the National Council of Jewish Women, and the World Union for Progressive Judaism—she preferred to be known simply as the wife of her illustrious husband. Their marriage of thirty-six years was a happy union of "two strong and individual personalities." She was far from being "the cautious stereotype of the organization wife"; she rejected compromise on issues of principle. No small part of Maurice's own courage and willingness to champion controversial causes "was drawn from the reservoirs of spirit of this remarkable woman who was always at his side—his stay and his support."

After Rosa's death, Eisendrath was barely able to function, cancelling public appearances. He felt helpless in the face of the myriad demands confronting him. Erwin Herman depicted the impact Rosa's passing had on Eisendrath:

> Maurice thought that his life had come to an end. Rosa did everything but breathe for him. She was his mentor and critic. He reviewed with her everything he wrote. Rosa's death . . . left him bereft not only of a lifemate but of the only support system that existed for him.

Maurice and Rosa had never cultivated personal friends, nor had he maintained close family ties. Four months after Rosa's death, Eisendrath appeared before the assembled delegates at the 1963 General Assembly and spoke about his personal loss:

> Surely there is none among this deeply understanding convocation of treasured friends and ardent co-workers who is not aware of the vast emptiness that yawns so painfully within my being; the gaping, hollowed-out void that has sucked the spark from my as yet seared and shackled spirit. Nor will any among you fail to forgive me for this personal indulgence; for prefacing whatever message may flow from my now long-silent lips and disquieted heart, with these words of mournful threnody over that precious soul who, during the now twenty years of our labors together within this Union, bore with me every frustration and failure, rejoiced in every forward stride which together we have made, hand-in-hand and heart-to-heart.

Approximately a year after Rosa's death, Eisendrath remarried. Rita Hands Greene had known "the Rabbi" since her student days at Holy Blossom Temple's religious school.

Eisendrath had confirmed her and officiated at her wedding to the actor Lorne Greene. The couple eventually divorced, but she was in occasional contact with the Union president. Upon hearing of Rosa's death, Rita wrote a consolation note that touched the grieving rabbi. They began a correspondence which led to their marriage in June 1964.

Eisendrath responded affectionately to Rita's two children, becoming an instant father and grandfather. An intelligent and vivacious woman, Rita enlivened his life. He admired her grace in large social gatherings, setting him at ease. Rita arranged for parties in their Manhattan apartment, introducing Maurice to cultural figures with whom he had little previous contact. She infused his life with renewed hope and purpose.

The year 1964 marked a second milestone for Eisendrath: the publication of *Can Faith Survive? The Thoughts and Afterthoughts of an American Rabbi*. The book, a collaborative effort with Albert Vorspan, [2] consisted of sixteen chapters on topics including Reform Judaism, Israel, pacifism, birth control, capital punishment, Jesus and Jewish-Christian relations, and the struggle to maintain one's religious faith in the midst of a secular world. Most chapters began with a lengthy quotation from a sermon or public address from his Toronto years, followed by an exposition of how his thinking on a particular subject had evolved or changed. UAHC publicity for the book carried the banner: "Rabbi Maurice Eisendrath asks . . . the questions that haunt Jewish life in America."

By 1965 few of Eisendrath's original staff remained at the Union's New York headquarters. Some left agreeably, others under a cloud of suspicion. Eugene Lipman, the first to leave, departed to become rabbi of Temple Sinai in Washington, D.C. A few years later Erwin Herman moved to California, where he directed the UAHC Pacific Southwest Region and served as national director of the regions. Eisendrath adjusted well to these changes.

The resignation of Eugene Borowitz, director of the Department of Education, however, infuriated the UAHC president. In Eisendrath's eyes, Borowitz defected to the enemy camp when he joined the faculty of the New York campus of HUC-JIR. Though the two were once close, after Borowitz left, their relationship was icy, at best.

Jay Kaufman's resignation in 1965 came as an even greater blow to Eisendrath. Kaufman, who was like a son to Eisendrath, had helped shape the Union's staff and operated as Eisendrath's "point man" in confronting numerous controversies. In 1957 Kaufman was rewarded by being elected to the newly created post of vice president. Ambitious, competent, and loyal, Kaufman had seemed the logical choice to succeed Eisendrath.

By the mid-1960s, Kaufman had been at the Union fifteen years. He wanted some assurance that he would be designated as Eisendrath's successor, but the UAHC president refused to guarantee Kaufman's succession. Perhaps he thought Kaufman was inappropriate for the job; though a highly intelligent man, he could be abrasive. It is also possible that by 1965 Eisendrath already favored as his successor Rabbi Alexander Schindler, former Union director of the New England Council and then director of the Education Department. Kaufman finally demanded a commitment from Eisendrath, threatening to resign. When Eisendrath made no attempt to dissuade him, Kaufman felt betrayed and left the Union to become executive vice president of B'nai Brith. Though Eisendrath did not fight to keep Kaufman on the Union's staff, he was deeply pained by the departure, as if he had lost a son. Rita Eisendrath recalls:

> When Jay left the Union Maurice was heartbroken. . . .
> I had the feeling the end of the world had come.

Albert Vorspan, the remaining member of Eisendrath's coordinating team, advanced to the newly created position of director of programs. Although his duties included coordinating and supervising the internal service departments of the Union, Vorspan was not considered a candidate for president because Eisendrath believed only a rabbi should head a Jewish religious organization. In 1967 Rabbi Alexander M. Schindler was named vice president of the Union, positioning him to become Eisendrath's successor.

Eisendrath was now sixty-five years old. The organization that had so benefited from his drive and energy now required much less of his attention. The Union's reputation was secure, its place in the councils of American Jewry undisputed.

The Reform movement, which he had striven to lead for twenty-five years, was undergoing significant changes in the mid-1960s. The Six-Day War had a profound effect on Jews throughout the world. Eisendrath expressed his solidarity with Israel in its "desperate, heroic struggle for survival," and exulted in her triumphant victory. He warned, however, that victorious Israel ought not become a vicarious Jewish identity for Reform Jews, who were withdrawing from the struggle for social justice in America. He attributed this "retreat" in part to the "deep hurt felt by Jews at the relative silence of the non-Jewish world in the face of Jewish suffering in Russia and Jewish peril in the Middle East." Nevertheless, he urged Jews to remain allied with black and Christian groups in the struggle to fight racism, environmental decay, and the Vietnam War. Yet he was unable to prevent some retreat by Jews from the social action front. Ruth Buchbinder, his secretary for many years, stated: "He never changed his liberal view . . . . He saw it going conservative and more and more to the right, and he saw himself, rightly or wrongly, as more and more isolated even from the world within which he operated."

In the late 1960s, Eisendrath felt increasingly uncomfortable with the growing traditionalism within the movement. Reform youths were experimenting with a variety of rituals—wearing *kippot* and *tallitot*, and observing *kashrut*. Eisendrath viewed this trend as an abandonment of rationalism. Some were even speaking of formulating a Reform Jewish *halachah*. He could support the idea of "certain fundamental, basic, minimal requirements incumbent upon the Reform Jew," but not *halachah*, denoting the immutability of Jewish law.

Eisendrath's health began to fail in 1970. He underwent three major surgeries within ten months, one to correct a strangulated hernia and two to treat back ailments. After a long and painful rehabilitation, he was able to progress from a wheelchair to an orthopedic cane.

Eisendrath kept up with Union affairs, reading his mail and dictating letters from the hospital. During his convalescence he even traveled abroad on Union business, but the organization was increasingly directed by Alexander Schindler, to whom Eisendrath had delegated authority.

Eisendrath had planned to retire in 1973, the Union's centennial year. Not surprisingly, the Union president worried about what he would do in retirement. Having been elected president of the World Union for Progressive Judaism, he planned to visit and assist congregations abroad. He also wanted to enroll in an ulpan program to improve his conversational Hebrew. He spoke of writing a book and working on an educational TV series.

Eisendrath was to hand over the reins of the Union formally to Alexander Schindler at the 1973 biennial in New York. As November grew near, Eisendrath concentrated on writing his final presidential sermon. The fire of protest still raged within him; his speech would advocate amnesty for draft evaders, arguing it was imperative to "manifest Jewish compassion toward those for whom it was ethically repugnant to rain down napalm, defoliation, and anti-personnel bombs upon the many innocent peasants below." In the wake of the Watergate Senate hearings, Eisendrath's text denounced President Nixon:

> How can we teach our children the Jewish values of honesty and compassion when "sneers and leers" are voiced not by press and TV, as alleged, but by those highest in office, an administration so indifferent to the dishonesty and pervasive corruption that have blackened the White House; so insensitive to the aged and the dispossessed, the disabled veterans of Vietnam; so obsessed with so-called "national security" as to defend the most unforgivable concealment and the most blatant fabrication? We have been led—or misled—to within an inch of a dictatorial police state.

Eisendrath had much to say about the Arab-Israel War, Zionism, Reform Judaism, Women, Youth. But he would never deliver his sermon. On Friday afternoon, on November 9, 1973, just hours before he was scheduled to speak, Maurice

Eisendrath died of a heart attack in his hotel room.

Rabbi Schindler announced the shocking news to the delegates, then read his predecessor's address to a muted and grieving assembly. On Sunday a memorial service was held in Central Synagogue, New York. Rabbi Roland Gittelsohn eulogized his longtime friend. He spoke of the public Eisendrath as "bold, brave, sometimes even a little brash, strong, resolute, courageous, always prophetic." Gittelsohn praised the private Maurice as "soft, tender, loving, considerate and passionate—always kind" to the privileged few who knew him.

Maurice Eisendrath's sudden death was wrenching and traumatic for his wife, his family and friends, and in a less tangible way, for the Union he had led for thirty years. Two decades have passed since he died. Time and distance permit one to establish a perspective on his life. The final chapter of this book will evaluate the man and his accomplishments.

EPILOGUE

Maurice Eisendrath received numerous awards, citations, degrees, and tributes that acknowledged his contributions as a leader of Reform Jewry and as a spokesman for international peace. These honors testify to the respect and appreciation bestowed upon him during his illustrious career. Signs of his influence remain. One can find an Eisendrath Auditorium at Holy Blossom Temple in Toronto, Canada. A bronze bust of Eisendrath stands in the lobby of the House of Living Judaism, New York, and on the tenth floor, his portrait decorates the boardroom. A Union-sponsored program for Israeli and American high school students bears his name—the Eisendrath International Exchange program, and students who spend a summer at the Religious Action Center are called Eisendrath interns. At each General Assembly, the Maurice N. Eisendrath "Bearer of Light" awards are bestowed by the UAHC for significant achievements in service to Reform Jewry, world Jewry, and the general community.

These traces of the man's life, however, fail to inform new generations of Eisendrath's legacy. Twenty years after his death, Eisendrath is scarcely remembered by the movement he led for thirty years. Today, only his family, his friends and associates, and historians recognize his contributions to Reform and to American Jewry.

This lack of recognition was in part a consequence of his awkwardness in social situations. Many perceived him as cold and authoritarian. He seemed more comfortable behind a lectern debating social issues than conversing one-to-one. He was uncomfortable in the chummy atmosphere of a party. Eisendrath could be kind and attentive to some people. He was warm and solicitous toward his family and a few associates, but he had difficulty communicating comfortably with the Jews he led. Throughout his life he held to the myth that the great leader of civilization must withdraw from society and climb the mountain alone in order to clarify his vision.

Eisendrath's climb through life was not easy. When he was sixteen he lost his father. His ambition to be a renowned Reform Jewish leader was in part fired by his desire to please the mother who supported him. He was just twenty-four when he began his duties as a congregational rabbi, and he hid his insecurities by adopting an aloof and formal manner. Only with Rosa was he able to let down his guard. She responded by protecting him, serving as a barrier between the public and her husband. This pattern continued throughout their married life. As he assumed ever greater responsibilities, Rosa became the primary repository of his emotions—a pattern he continued with his second wife, Rita. A man who was unable to project warmth is not warmly remembered.

Perhaps Eisendrath is not recalled much these days because leadership styles have changed. In his time, donning the prophetic mantle was seen as the chief responsibility of a rabbi. Rabbis utilized their pulpits for addressing not only their congregants but American Jewry as a whole. Stephen S. Wise, Edward Israel, and Abba Hillel Silver were national leaders. But the postwar period brought dramatic changes in the Reform rabbinate. The rabbi, as leader of a congregation, could no longer claim to be the sole, legitimate representative of American Jewry. Federations challenged the primacy of the synagogue, gaining influence through the control of communal funding. Eisendrath combatted this trend, deploring secular agencies that sought to represent Jewish interests.

Though in title Eisendrath was the president of a national

organization, he never ceased to think of himself as a pulpit rabbi. The Union was his pulpit, and he was the rabbi of all Reform Jewry. His "State of Our Union" address was fashioned as a High Holy Day sermon to a continental congregation. As a rabbi, he felt it was his duty to speak his mind, to point the finger, to demand action. He was never more attuned to his conception of Judaism and his role as a rabbi than when he thundered against the sin of segregation or decried American involvement in the Vietnam War.

We can admire Eisendrath's unwillingness to compromise on issues of conscience. He courageously battled the reactionary elements in his movement and in society at large. He had a remarkable ability to communicate his passion for justice. Under his leadership, the General Assembly passed a number of progressive resolutions. Yet today the biblical prophets are no longer widely viewed as representing the essence of Judaism. Though it is important to express our convictions on social issues, we are skeptical of those who utilize a few passages from a particular prophet as justification for a course of action. As noted in the 1976 Centenary Perspective of the CCAR, today we listen to a plurality of voices—"lawgivers and prophets, historians and poets . . . rabbis and teachers, philosophers and mystics"—gifted Jews of every age that speak to us with wisdom. And whereas in the past a rabbi such as Eisendrath could serve as an uncompromising voice of conscience from atop the mountain, today many Jews want rabbis to display intimacy and not distance, empathy, not rebuke. It may be that Eisendath is not widely remembered because the mode of rabbinic leadership he espoused is no longer desired by Reform Jews in the 1990s.

Eisendrath is remembered today primarily for his accomplishments as president of the UAHC. It is no exaggeration to say that he was the most important organizational leader of the Reform movement since Isaac Mayer Wise. Eisendrath perceived, along with others, that for the UAHC to flourish it must harness the energy of the new leaders of American Jews: the second generation of American-born Jews of Eastern European background. He modified his views on Zionism and the importance of ritual in Judaism because of the exigencies of his day.

Yet Eisendrath was no mere reflection of his era. He was a doer and a builder. The transfer of the Union from Cincinnati to New York, the gathering in of hundreds of thousands of new congregants, the enlargement of the Union's budget and staff, the building of the Religious Action Center in Washington, D.C., and the Union's gain in prestige and influence in American Jewish life were all made possible by Maurice Eisendrath.

How can a man who accomplished so much in his lifetime be scarcely remembered today? HUC historian Dr. Jacob Rader Marcus comments:

> Goethe says somewhere that "nobody is remembered sixty years after his death." Of course Goethe was an exception. Who remembers Kohler? Who remembers Morgenstern? Who remembers Glueck? Nobody is remembered . . . . It is perfectly normal that a man is forgotten except by the historian who makes a special study.

Dr. Marcus may be right. Yet his answer engenders another question: Why make a special study of a person's life? The purpose of a biography is to assess honestly an individual's life so that we may ultimately learn about ourselves and the human endeavor. One primary lesson to be learned from this biography of Eisendrath is that he was eminently human. He had strengths and foibles. He loved some and loathed others. He was ambitious and set goals—some of which he realized.

Like so many people, he had a dream of a more just and peaceful world. What distinguished Eisendrath was the intensity and magnitude of his determination to realize that dream. Most people are content to mouth words of hope for a better world. Eisendrath despised pieties, for his dreams beckoned him to act. Toward the end of his life, Maurice Eisendrath was asked, "For what would you like to be best remembered?" After a long pause, he said, "That I helped move humanity and Jewry one scintilla forward toward the messianic era." His answer wholly reflects the man. He was a Jewish leader, both altruistic and vain, with a passionate concern about his people and humanity. Until the day he died, a fire of truth still burned within him.

FOOTNOTES

Introduction

1.   Rabbi Eugene Lipman in recorded interview conducted by author, Washington, D.C., June 8, 1983.

CHAPTER 1 *"Eisey": 1902-1926*

1.   My favorite excerpt from a column in the *HUC Monthly* written by "Schlemiehl" is from the November 1924 issue, pages 12–13: "I would like to give you an impression of the Freshman class, Abe, but space does not permit. . . . They have one thing in common and that is 'chutzpah.' Their favorite tricks are hiding the paddle and locking the dormitory at night (with me on the outside), pouring water from the windows upon the heads of sedate seniors, calling for bacon with their eggs at breakfast, kidding Dr. Cohon and challenging the faculty to a golf tournament, singing college songs of twenty-seven different colleges simultaneously while holding a shirt tail parade on the second floor, etc., etc. Yes, the boys are a bit playful, Abe, but then boys will be boys especially at the Hebrew Union College."

2.   *HUC Monthly*, February 1919, p. 94.

3.   Maurice Eisendrath, *Can Faith Survive? The Thoughts and Afterthoughts of an American Rabbi* (New York, 1964), p. 5. Eisendrath received a Bachelor of Arts degree from the University of Cincinnati in 1925 and was elected to Phi Beta Kappa.

4.   In the years following his student days, Eisendrath seemed to enjoy a cordial relationship with Morgenstern. A perusal of the Morgenstern-Eisendrath correspondence (AJA Hebrew Union College Collection) reveals that they were in touch on a variety of issues like Moses Buttenwieser's premature retirement in 1935 and funding for the Institute of Jewish Studies in Warsaw. Morgenstern warmly commended Eisendrath's conference sermon at the 1937 CCAR convention, adding: "I need not tell you that your own views and mine coincide completely." Letter of Julian Morgenstern to Maurice Eisendrath, June 8, 1937.

CHAPTER 2 *Pulpit and Politics: 1926-1943*

1.   Harrison E. Salisbury, "West Virginia: Battleground for Democrats," *New York Times,* April 29, 1960, noted that until the mid-seventeen hundreds, Roman Catholics were legally barred from Virginia. Salisbury's article can be found in Abraham I. Shinedling, *West Virginia Jewry* (Philadelphia, 1963), vol. 1.

2.   This figure based upon statistics given in Stuart Rosenberg, "Canada's Jews: The Sacred and the Profane," *Conservative Judaism,* vol. 24, no. 3 (Spring 1970), p. 35. In contrast to 150,000 Jews in Canada, there were over 4 million Jews in the United States.

3.   For a well-drawn account of the growth of Fascist movements in Canada as well as the relations between Canada and Germany in the 1930s see Lita-Rose Betcherman, *The Swastika and the Maple Leaf* (Toronto, 1975).

4.   Irving Abella and Harold E. Troper, " 'The Line Must Be Drawn Somewhere' ": Canada and Jewish Refugees, 1933–1939," in *The Canadian Jewish Mosaic,* William Shaffir, Morton Weinfeld, and Irving Cotler, eds. (Toronto, 1981), p. 51.

5.   Dr. Jacob Rader Marcus in recorded interview conducted by the author, Cincinnati, Ohio, August 9, 1983.

CHAPTER 3 *At the Union's Helm: 1943-1951*

1.   Article II of UAHC Constitution, 1873.

2.   Michael A. Meyer, "A Centennial History," in *Hebrew Union College– Jewish Institute of Religion at One Hundred Years,* Samuel Karff, ed. (Cincinnati, 1976), pp. 173–174.

3.   "Words cannot adequately express the profound wrench with which I tear myself away from Toronto this week, even though I anticipate being back with you by Pesach, and notwithstanding the fact that we all hope that my leave of absence will be of brief duration. However, it is with genuine heartache that I turn, even for the nonce, to other tasks." Eisendrath in *Holy Blossom Bulletin,* March 26, 1943. In the debate regarding Eisendrath and the Union post, it is curious to note that in December of 1942, just a month before he became the Union's interim director, the Eisendraths moved into a new home in Toronto.

4.   M. Eisendrath interview.

5.   For the complete text of the resolution see Howard Greenstein, *Turning Point: Zionism and Reform Judaism* (Ann Arbor, 1981), p. 177.

6.   *Ibid.,* p. 97.

7.   *Ibid.,* p. 69.

8.   "Why the Union Belongs in New York," *Liberal Judaism* 16 (October 1948), p. 40.

CHAPTER 4 *Revival and Expansion: 1951-1963*

1.   These figures are from *Decade of Progress, the Report of the President of the UAHC to the Executive Board,* October 24, 1953, p. 3. In his report, Eisendrath referred to the growth of the Union membership "from approximately 50,000 members to well over 150,000." In 1948, in his *State of Our Union* address (p. 5), he indicated that the Union in 1943 comprised some three hundred congregations with a member-ship of some sixty thousand families. By 1948, Eisendrath stated that the number had risen to four hundred congregations with more than one hundred thousand families enrolled in the Union.

2.   Nathan Glazer, *American Judaism* (1972), pp. 116–117.

3.   Over the years, Ruth Buchbinder had a very productive and affectionate rela-tionship with her boss. In a letter to him written on May 19, 1965, she stated, "I have said to you in the past, and I gladly repeat now, that I admire your honesty and integrity. I do not always sympathize with your views nor agree with your conclu-sions. But I am a confirmed respecter of your struggles with yourself and, poor man, with your staff as you go through your special form of self-torture to arrive at decisions you consider necessary, just, compassionate and right. I am a constantly awed admir-er of your willingness to submit your own thoughts and feelings to the not always gen-tle gaze of others. I think it's a hard way to make a living, but I think it's enriching for those involved. And every third day I'm glad that I've been involved. I think you're an 'honest to God' rabbi—though there are moments when I wish you weren't." Ruth Buchbinder in interview conducted by Rabbi Edward Paul Cohn, New York, New York, April 2, 1981, transcript deposited in the AJA.

4.   Evidently it was common practice among the staff to organize at each biennial a pool as to how long Eisendrath's State of Our Union speeches would last. Winners usually chose over 60 minutes.

5.   In the citation awarded to Eisendrath by the Religious Heritage of America, he was commended for being a "fearless defender of justice, leader of the UAHC, champion of civil rights, the rebirth of Israel, international understanding, aid to needy nations, pioneer statesman, and dedicated prophet of the Holy One." AJA Eisendrath Collection.

6.   Meyer, "A Centennial History," pp. 201–202. Nelson Glueck, in his "President's Report to the Board of Governors of the Hebrew Union College," January 22, 1958, responded to the charge that the proper relationship of the College to the Union was that of a child to a parent: "Since when must the child be utterly subservient to the parent, and what kind of parent attempts to exact that kind of obedience in this day and age, or ever could in any age? And besides, how long does it take for a child to grow up? This child is only three years younger than the parent and is now 83 years old. Some child!"

CHAPTER 5 *"With Moral Indignation and Righteous Protest"*

1.   The CCAR already had a Commission on Social Justice. In 1918 the CCAR ratified a social ethics platform that is noteworthy for its progressivism. Revisions were adopted in 1920 and 1928. See Roland Gittelsohn, "The Conference Stands on Social Justice and Civil Rights," in *Retrospect and Prospect: Essays in Commemoration of the Seventy-fifth Anniversary of the Founding of the CCAR, 1889–1964*, Bertram Korn, ed. (New York, 1965), p. 88. Also see Michael A. Meyer, *Response to Modernity, A History of the Reform Movement in Judaism* (Oxford 1988), pp. 309–313.

2.   Ben Firestone, "Decision on Social Action," *Congress Bi-weekly,* December 11, 1961, p. 12.

3.   *Ibid.*

4.   For insights about the organized Jewish community's response to the Vietnam War, I thank Rabbi Irwin Zeplowitz. See his rabbinic thesis, "Jewish Attitudes Toward the Vietnam War" (Cincinnati: Hebrew Union College – Jewish Institute of Religion, 1984).

CHAPTER 6 *"Jesus—Man of My People"*

1.   "Ecumenism," *Time,* November 29, 1963, p. 51.

2.   Rabbi Norman Lamm, "Reform Leader Castigated for Church Schema Reaction," *Rabbinical Council Record,* vol. 10, no. 2 (January 1964), pp. 3 and 4, AJA Eisendrath Collection.

3.   *Congress Bi-weekly* (American Jewish Congress), December 2, 1963, p. 4, AJA Eisendrath Collection.

4.   Rabbi Leonard Winograd, letter to the editor, *National Jewish Post,* December 27, 1963, AJA Eisendrath Collection.

5.   Rabbi Balfour Brickner quoted in *Newsweek,* "The Jews and Jesus," December 2, 1963.

6.   Rabbi Sanford Seltzer, "Reactions to Jesus in the Reform Rabbinate," rabbinic thesis, is an excellent resource for grasping the differing trends in the Reform movement's understanding of Jesus.

7.   Professor Samuel Sandmel, quoted in S. Seltzer, "Reactions to Jesus," p. 12. The preceding quotes from Dr. J. Morgenstern and Rabbi M. Raisin are also from Seltzer (p. 30 and p. 14).

CHAPTER 7 *Slowed Steps: 1963-1973*

1.   Buchbinder interview.

2.   *Can Faith Survive?* (New York: McGraw-Hill Book Company, 1964) was a collaborative effort by Eisendrath and Albert Vorspan. Eisendrath and Vorspan worked out the outline for a chapter; then Vorspan drafted the chapter; then the two together re-worked it.

BIBLIOGRAPHY

AMERICAN JEWISH ARCHIVES MATERIALS, *Cincinnati, Ohio*

    Maurice Eisendrath Collection

    Solomon Freehof Collection

    Robert Goldman Collection

    Nelson Glueck Correspondence

    Hebrew Union College Collection

    Union of American Hebrew Congregations Collection

INTERVIEWS

Borowitz, Eugene. Professor of Education and Jewish Religious Thought, HUC-JIR, New York. Recorded interview conducted by author in Port Washington, New York, August 18, 1983. In author's possession.

Buchbinder, Ruth. Interview conducted by Rabbi Edward Paul Cohn, New York, New York, April 2, 1981. Transcript deposited in the American Jewish Archives.

Eisendrath, Rita. Recorded interview conducted by author in Purdys, New York, August 16, 1983. In author's possession.

Evans, Jane. Director Emeritus, National Federation of Temple Sisterhoods. Recorded interview conducted by author in New York, New York, August 17, 1983. In author's possession.

Glaser, Joseph. Executive Vice President, Central Conference of American Rabbis. "Remembrances of Maurice Eisendrath." New York, New York, 1983. Microcassette sent originally to Rabbi Edward Paul Cohn. In author's possession.

Herman, Erwin. Director Emeritus, UAHC Pacific Southwest Council. "Reflections on Maurice Eisendrath." Lake San Marcos, California, Fall 1983. Tape in author's possession.

Hess, Marjory and Nathaniel E. Recorded interview conducted by Rabbi Eugene Borowitz in Port Washington, New York, November 3, 1983. In author's possession.

Kleinman, Solomon. Rabbi Emeritus, Temple Ahavat Shalom, Northridge, California. Recorded interview conducted by author July 1, 1983. In author's possession.

Lipman, Eugene. Rabbi Emeritus, Temple Sinai, Washington, D.C. Recorded interview conducted by author in Washington, D.C., June 8, 1983. In author's possession.

Marcus, Jacob Rader. Milton and Hattie Kutz Distinguished Service Professor of American Jewish History, HUC-JIR, Cincinnati. Recorded interview conducted by author in Cincinnati, Ohio, August 9, 1983. In author's possession.

Vorspan, Albert. Vice President, Union of American Hebrew Congregations. Not recorded interview conducted by author, Washington, D.C., June 6, 1983.

Zeldin, Isaiah. Rabbi, Stephen S. Wise Temple, Los Angeles, California. Recorded interview conducted by author, Los Angeles, California, July 1, 1983. In author's possession.

PRIMARY SOURCES: *Articles, Books, Interviews, Reports, Sermons, Speeches by Maurice N. Eisendrath, in Chronological Order*

1925   "The Supremacy of Self." *HUC Monthly* 12 (February 28), pp. 2–6.

1926   "Fulness of Life." *HUC Monthly* 13 (May 29), p. 20.
"Universalism and Particularism in the Priestly Code with Special Reference to Ezekiel and Deutero-Isaiah." Rabbinic thesis, HUC, Cincinnati.

1936   "Building a Co-operative Commonwealth in Zion." Holy Blossom Pulpit (sermon delivered January 19).
"If Jesus Had Not Come." Holy Blossom Pulpit (sermon delivered April 12).

1937   "Retreat or Advance?" Sermon delivered before the CCAR, Columbus, Ohio, May 29. Klau Library, HUC-JIR, Cincinnati.

1939   *The Never Failing Stream.* Toronto.

1942   "Comments on the CCAR Jewish Army Resolution." *CCAR Yearbook,* p. 177.

1943   "Toronto." *Universal Jewish Encyclopedia,* vol. 10.
"For Such a Time as This." Founder's Day Address, HUC, Cincinnati, Ohio, March 27. Klau Library.

1944   Report of the Director to the Executive Board of the UAHC. November 26. Klau Library.

1946   *Made In America: The Story of Reform Judaism in the United States.* UAHC. Klau Library.
"The State of Our Union." Cincinnati, March 3. Klau Library.

1948   "The State of Our Union." Boston, November 14. Klau Library.

1950   "The Unthinkable Has Happened." *The Sentinel,* September 28.

1953   "The State of Our Union." New York, April 19. Klau Library.
"Decade of Progress." Report of the President to the UAHC Executive Board. October 24. AJA.
"A Jewish Platform of Good Will." National Conference of Christians and Jews. Klau Library.

1955   "The State of Our Union." Los Angeles, February 13. Klau Library.
"Challenge to the Jew: To Set the Right in the Earth." Delivered at the meeting of the World Union for Progressive Judaism, Paris, July 4. Klau Library.

1956   Report of the President to the UAHC Executive Board. October 20. AJA.

1959   Report of the President to the UAHC Board of Trustees. May 23. AJA.
"The State of Our Union." Miami Beach, November 15. AJA.

1960   Report of the President to the UAHC Board of Trustees. June 11–12. AJA.

1961   "Bearers of the Light." Baccalaureate Address, Ordination Service, HUC, Cincinnati, Ohio, June 3. Klau Library.
"The State of Our Union." Washington, D.C., November 12. Klau Library.

1963   "The State of Our Union." Chicago, November 16. Klau Library.
"Memorial Tribute to Felix Levy." *CCAR Yearbook,* pp. 129–130.

1964   Report of the President to the UAHC Board of Trustees. November 21. AJA.
Can Faith Survive? The Thoughts and Afterthoughts of an American Rabbi. New York.

Jewry and Jesus of Nazareth. Co-authored with James Parkes. Great Britain.

1965   Report of the President to the UAHC Board of Trustees.   May 22. AJA.

    "The State of Our Union." San Francisco, November 14. AJA.

1966   Report of the President to the UAHC Board of Trustees.   December 3. AJA.

1967   Report of the President to the UAHC Board of Trustees. May 28. Klau Library.

    "The State of Our Union." Montreal, November 12. Klau Library.

1968   Report of the President to the UAHC Board of Trustees.   November 24. AJA.

1972   Recorded interview conducted by Rabbi Daniel Syme. New York, New York, May 10. Deposited in the AJA.

1973   Presidential sermon. New York, November 9. Klau Library.

SECONDARY SOURCES

Abella, Irving, and Troper, Harold E. "'The Line Must Be Drawn Somewhere': Canada and Jewish Refugees, 1933–1939." In *The Canadian Jewish Mosaic,* Shaffir, William; Weinfeld, Morton; and Cotler, Irwin, eds. Toronto, 1981.

American Jewish Archives. "Union of American Hebrew Congregations Centennial: A Documentary." *American Jewish Archives* 25 (Cincinnati, April 1973).

American Jewish Yearbook 31 (Philadelphia, 1929), pp. 302, 307.

American Judaism 1–16 (New York, 1951–1967).

Bamberger, Henry. "Some Difficulties in Dialogue." *Judaism* 32 (Spring 1983), pp. 176–183.

Belkin, Simon. *Through Narrow Gates.* Montreal, 1966.

Betcherman, Lita-Rose. *The Swastika and the Maple Leaf.* Toronto, 1975.

Borowitz, Eugene. "Rethinking the Reform Jewish Theory of Social Action." *Journal of Reform Judaism* (Fall 1980), pp. 1–19.

Cohn, Edward Paul. "Reason for Hope: The Life and Works of Rabbi Maurice N. Eisendrath." Doctor of Ministry thesis, Kansas City, Missouri, 1983.

CCAR. *CCAR Resolutions 1889–1974.* Edited by Elliot Stevens and Simeon Glaser. New York, 1975.

Justice and Peace: A Statement of Principles. New York, 1960.

Elazar, Daniel. *Community and Polity.* Philadelphia, 1980.

Firestone, Ben. "Decision on Social Action." *Congress Bi-weekly* 28 (December 11, 1961), pp. 11–12.

Gittelsohn, Roland. "Eulogy for Maurice Eisendrath." November 11, 1973.

"Memorial Tribute to Maurice N. Eisendrath." *CCAR Yearbook* 1974, pp. 205–206.

"The Conference Stands on Social Justice and Civil Rights." In *Retrospect and Prospect: Essays in Commemoration of the Seventy-fifth Anniversary of the Founding of the CCAR, 1889–1964.* Edited by Bertram Korn, New York, 1965.

Glazer, Nathan. *American Judaism.* 2d rev. ed. Chicago, 1972.

Greenstein, Howard. *Turning Point: Zionism and Reform Judaism.* Ann Arbor, 1981.

Hirsch, Richard G. "Memorial Tribute to Jay Kaufman." *CCAR Yearbook* 1972, pp. 171–174.

Holy Blossom Bulletin 5–19 (Toronto, 1929–1943).

HUC Monthly 4–13 (Cincinnati, 1917–1926).

Hyman, Ralph. "Holy Blossom Temple's History." *125 Years: Holy Blossom Temple Anniversary Album.* Toronto, 1981.

Kage, Joseph. *With Faith and Thanksgiving.* Montreal, 1962.

Kayfetz, Ben G. "Canada." *Encyclopaedia Judaica.* 1972 edition.

Klein, Gary M. "Nelson Glueck: A Leader of Liberal Jewry." Rabbinic thesis, HUC-JIR, Cincinnati, 1975.

Liberal Judaism 11–19 (New York, 1943–1951).

Martin, Bernard. *Movements and Issues in American Judaism: An Analysis and Sourcebook of Developments Since 1945.* Westport, 1978.

Meyer, Michael A. "A Centennial History." In *Hebrew Union College-Jewish Institute of Religion at One Hundred Years,* edited by Samuel Karff, pp. 1–283. Cincinnati, 1976.

"Reform Judaism." In *Movements and Issues in American Judaism: An Analysis and Sourcebook of Developments Since 1945,* edited by Bernard Martin, pp. 158–170. Westport, 1978.

_____. *Response to Modernity: A History of the Reform Movement in Judaism.* New York, 1988.

Plaut, W. Gunther. *The Growth of Reform Judaism.* New York, 1965.

Rosenberg, Stuart E. "Canada's Jews: An Overview." *Judaism* 20 (Fall 1971), pp. 476–489.

"Canada's Jews: The Sacred and the Profane." *Conservative Judaism* 24 (Spring 1970), pp. 34–44.

Rudin, Jacob. "President's Message." *CCAR Yearbook,* 1958.

Seltzer, Sanford. "Reactions to Jesus in the Reform Rabbinate." Rabbinic thesis, HUC-JIR, Cincinnati, 1959.

Shinedling, Abraham. *West Virginia Jewry: Origins and History 1850-1958.* Philadelphia, 1963.

Temkin, Sefton D. "A Century of Reform Judaism in America." *American Jewish Yearbook* (Philadelphia, 1973), pp. 3-75.

Union of American Hebrew Congregations. *A Prince Has Fallen in Israel.* 1973.
Constitution and By-Laws of the UAHC. As amended, October 1969.
Twenty Questions on Reform Judaism and Social Action. New York, 1961.
Where We Stand: Social Action Resolutions of the UAHC, 1873–1980. New York, 1980.

Urofsky, Melvin. *A Voice That Spoke for Justice.* Albany, 1982.

Vorspan, Albert. "In Memoriam: Rosa Brown Eisendrath." *American Judaism* 13 (Fall 1963), p. 4.

Vorspan, Albert, and Lipman, Eugene J. *Justice and Judaism.* New York, 1956.

Warschauer, Heinz. *The Story of Holy Blossom Temple.* Toronto, 1956.

Washington Hebrew Congregation. *A Statement of Principle for Reform Jewish Congregations.* Washington, D.C., February 15, 1961.

Weinfeld, Morton; Shaffir, William; and Cotler, Irwin, eds. *The Canadian Jewish Mosaic.* Toronto, 1981.

Zeplowitz, Irwin A. "Jewish Attitudes Toward the Vietnam War." Rabbinic thesis, HUC-JIR, Cincinnati, 1984.

APPENDIX:"THE STATE OF OUR UNION"

MESSAGE OF THE PRESIDENT TO THE

45TH GENERAL ASSEMBLY OF

UNION OF AMERICAN HEBREW CONGREGATIONS

Miami Beach, Florida, November 15, 1959

RABBI MAURICE N. EISENDRATH

THE STATE OF OUR UNION

B'RUCHIM HABOIM B'SHEM ADONOY. "BLESSED ARE YE WHO COME IN THE name of the Lord." Most earnestly do I pray that it *is* in the name of God that we gather in such overflowing numbers here beside these sun and sea-splashed sands. To this truly "fabulous" place, whither multitudes swarm for physical relaxation and reinvigoration, we have come for spiritual refreshment and moral resurgence, hopefully to seek out the way of the Lord.

The Constitution of our Union provides that its President shall render a Report to this Biennial Assembly on the progress and program of this Union. It does not specify whether it shall be written or oral. In the past, it has been both. This night, however, you will be handed a written Report which will rehearse for you the phenomenal development of this great Union: The formation of new congregations at the rate of about one every other week, the veritable miracle of our Youth, religiously reborn through our NFTY camps and conclaves, the deepening content of our program of education from nursery school through adulthood, the march of our regional organization, the maturation of our search for social action. Of this—and so much more—you will read with well-warranted pride that you are a part of this vital and vigorous movement of American Reform Judaism.

But there is at least one conspicuous omission in this printed Report, an omission which may best be described by a rabbinic commentary on the Sidrah, *Lech l'cho*, which was read in all our synagogues just yesterday. The phrase "Lech l'cho," our sages point out, occurs but twice in the entire Bible, both times in this same Parasha, in this tale of Abraham: *Lech l'cho me-artz'cho*, "Go forth *from* thy land, *from* thy birthplace," it declares. And then, it adds, *Lech l'cho el eretz umimoladet'cho, ha-Moriah*—"Go forth *to* the land of Moriah." And our rabbis avidly debated the comparative importance of "going *from*" or "going *to*" a given place. After long deliberation they concluded that each is of utmost significance. The printed Report that you will receive traces our triumphant advance *from* the time we last convened. But, equally important is the goal *to* which we are directing all these energies. More urgent still is the necessity of *evaluating* all our present activity in the light of our ultimate destiny as Jews, as Americans, as children of this mid-twentieth century atomic age.

It will be the purpose, therefore, of this message, to attempt to examine collectively, as rigorously as we do individually at the Holy Season, whether as a movement, as an organization, we are all that we claim to be; whether we are justifying the numerical strength of which we, sometimes a bit too vaingloriously, boast; whether we are measuring up, with all the potential spiritual power that might be at our disposal, to the unprecedented challenge of our day; to "search and try our ways and to return," as individuals and as a group, "unto the Lord, our God." It is, then, in this sense that I pray that it is not presumptuous to echo the age-old greeting of our forebears: "Blessed are ye who come in the name of the Lord."

This is the first time in more than a half-century that this nigh unto ninety-year-old Union of ours has met in this Southeast Region—teeming with new vigor and vitality. We meet in this magnificent Fontainebleau Hotel—one of the few places now large enough to accommodate our ever-increasing legion of delegates. With consummate pride we often say that they "don't hardly make accommodations big enough no more" for our expanding, exploding Reform constituency. But surely, there come moments of gnawing anxiety when we begin to comprehend the meaning of that phrase "the curse of bigness"; when we wonder whether, amid all this phenomenal adding of member to member, congregation to congregation, region to region, staff to staff, we may not be failing to impart to those who, for a multiplicity of reasons are flocking to our fold, the true import of our Jewish faith in general and of our Reform Judaism in particular; to wonder whether all this "spiritual euphoria" we are presently experiencing may not be, as some have suggested, but a "skin-deep, status-seeking revivalism," whether all this frantic, frenetic, frenzied hurricane of organizationalism does not whirl around the eye of an empty and emasculated center; does not, like all hurricanes spin off a host of minor hectic whirlwinds of theater parties and raffles and bingoes—good for fund-raising but signifying little, if anything, of spiritual content.

Mind you, I am not among those spiritual snobs who frown upon numerical growth because they prefer to keep Reform a kind of comfortable little family compact, and who assert with a supercilious sneer, "When I go to temple there's hardly anyone I know any more." Surely, if we believe that Reform Judaism has anything whatsoever to offer to our time, we dare not disdain to win as many cohorts as possible to our banner, whatever may be their motivation, be it prompted by Erich Fromm's thesis of "belongingness"; suburbia's craving for conformity with the "community set-up"—or what not. If the Talmud tells us that "even if one enters into an activity for an ulterior motive, it is still possible to arrive at a correct principle" then who are we to spurn these avid neophytes or fail to be challenged by the potential spiritual opportunity which our vast numbers offer?

So I say welcome; thrice welcome to all who seek our midst. But these words of warmest welcome must be accompanied by the inescapable responsibility to make known to such newcomers that it is no religion of convenience, that it is no regimen of do-and-know-nothingness which they have joined. Libelous, indeed, are the words of our detractors, from those fanatics in mid-nineteenth century Germany who sought to betray the founders of our Reform faith to the government of their time, to Herman Wouk today and his flippant parody of Reform whereby, in his recent *This Is My God*, he defames us as "an undemanding religion, freed of any ritual inconvenience," as a kind of down-sliding "cascade" from the exalted heights of Orthodoxy. Some cascade! From debating whether a mohel shall draw off the blood of circumcision with his lips or with a glass tube, as is seriously discussed in a recent issue of the Orthodox periodical *Perspective*; from how near to or how far from the "shul" one may surreptitiously drive one's car on Yom Tov or Shabos; from to bathe or not to bathe in the "mikveh"—some cascade from all this which ofttimes passes for Judaism to the prophetic mandate to "cease to do evil, learn to do good" which is the essence and emphasis of our search and aspiration in Reform Judaism! Some cascade! From Wouk's apotheosis of the "fireworks" of Bar Mitzvah as a kind of Jewish version of the "American coming out party," to the "Thou shalts" and "Thou shalt nots" of our moral law. The demands and the commands of Reform Judaism do indeed comprise the most compelling challenge which men have been called upon to confront—especially at this awesome hour of crisis and decision when our Reform Judaism, Judaism, all religion, face new frontiers such as we have never known before.

Now there are those who deny any such *Chidush*, anything so altogether novel in our time. Quoting the cynical Ecclesiastes they insist that "there is nothing new under the sun." They insist that the "good old religion" which fortified our forebears to face the destruction of the Temple, the devastation of their beloved land of Israel, the Crusades and Inquisition, ought to suffice for our time as well. Perhaps so. But to compare the universe of our fathers with the era in which we find ourselves today is to indulge in sheer "kinderspiel." The prophet, Joel, may have come close to describing our own time when he presaged a day of darkness wherein, in words harrowingly contemporary, he lamented, "The grains shrivel; the barns are broken down; the beasts pant for the water; the brooks are dried up; the corn is withered—and the flame hath set ablaze all the trees of the fields." And yet, even these prophets of doom dared always to predict that a *Sh'or yoshuv*, "a remnant," would return "to plant and to build." In their most apocalyptic of visions they could not foresee a time when a single bomb might pulverize whole cities into radioactive rubble in a matter of a few hours and reduce the whole earth to irradiated dust in a matter of days. They may have inveighed against those who "sold the needy for a pair of shoes," but they could believe still that man was but "little lower than the angels and crowned with honor and glory." In their most melancholy of moods they could not have envisaged the denigration of the individual in this age of automation whereby once proud and thinking man is increasingly reduced to a finger-print in a file, a punch card in an IBM calculator, a mote of dust on a conveyor belt monotonously stamped by the same die into exchangeable, and hence, expendable parts.

Can Reform Judaism confront such new frontiers of personal debasement and possible imminent world destruction, before which man feels, as never before, utterly dwarfed and impotent, a Don Quixote tilting at gigantic windmills and skyrocketing missiles? Can Reform Judaism find the spiritual resources and moral reserves to transform Don Quixote into David, diminutive still but armed with the sling of such an indomitable spirit as might yet slay the Goliath of our rocket and racket-ridden age?

Such is the first new frontier which I would ask this Assemblage to confront. Let us "search and try our ways," that we may return in sincerity and truth "unto the Lord our God"—the genesis, the source of all that we are and hope to be. There are Jews, we must frankly confess, who deny any such necessity and who, if we be scrupulously honest, give at least some credence to the charge recently leveled against us in a responsible Christian publication, that we contemporary Jews "scarcely have a religion . . . that even those who cherish a strong sense of the Judaic tradition often seem to hold it as a sort of superintense patriotism without personal awareness of God or the religious teachings of their forefathers." While some of us may have been tempted to shout "anti-Semite" at the writer of those words, if we truly search and try our ways and examine that which prompts each one of us to maintain his Jewish identity, to contribute to UJA or Bonds for Israel, or even to join a synagogue, must we not, in the innermost recesses of our being, confess that sometimes, at least, it *is* an ethnic and national chauvinism, a loyalty to the peoplehood of Israel alone, to the statehood of Israel alone, to the body of Israel rather than to its soul or teachings or moral *mitsvos* that motivate our identification? This is not an altogether ignoble motivation. On the contrary, it has wrought much worthy enterprise. It prompts us to buy by the wholesale and to read by the millions the latest best seller *Exodus*, but it attains Zion via a short-cut that by-passes Sinai. It is good, but it is not good enough. It succors Jews—and for that we are deeply grateful. But it may not save Judaism.

This deification of Israel, state or people, explodes in a multitude of contexts. I heard it—of all places, this summer past from the lips of an Israeli at the deliberations of the World Union for Progressive Judaism. "Only the establishment of the State of Israel," he asserted, "gives warrant to Jewish existence, to Jewish sacrifice and striving!" I read it in a recent issue of a popular magazine wherein a Jew who recounted how he was once booted out of Germany had recently returned to the Vaterland after some years in Israel and now insisted that never again would he be made to flee his native land because, whereas, formerly "They" (the Germans) "thought it was easy to chase a Jew away because they always believed that we were yellow, they don't know what *Israel* can teach a Jew." I am not disparaging what Israel can teach a Jew, and what its restoration has meant to many, even to most Jews—and sensitive non-Jews too; but I am challenging this superficial denial of the whole destiny of the Jew which affirms that it was God, and faith in God and fortitude because of God, which gave the Jew in centuries past, are capable of imparting to the Jew of today, similar spiritual courage and moral daring: A Job, insisting "though He slay me, yet will I trust in Him"; an Akiba, burning at the stake; a Solomon Ibn Verga, proclaiming *Ribon ho-Olomim harbeh ato oseh she-e-ezov dati*—"Master of the Universe, though Thou art doing much to force me to forsake my faith, nothing that Thou hast brought upon me will do so"; and myriads who in our own time faced the ghoulish threat of the death chambers with the *Ani ma-amin*, but "I still believe" on their lips; an Anne Frank, huddled in her hidden attic, yet affirming, "I believe that men are good at heart." Surely these, renowned or humble, required neither blood-bond nor soil to keep them from being "yellow," from fleeing like cowards, from feeling that sense of inferiority which so many today insist that only flags and frontiers, rather than an exalted faith, can dissipate.

To find again this erstwhile indomitable faith of the spirit must be the paramount task of our Union as we face this new frontier of our bewildered personal lives. All the magnificent new temples which so many of us have sacrificially reared, all the multiplication of our organizational machinery, all our vast accretion of numbers, all the training our rabbis have received, all the clatter of our crowded congregational calendars, all the services which our Union renders, all our Union's fevered appeal for funds, even the present desperate entreaty by the eminent President of the Hebrew Union College-Jewish Institute of Religion, my cherished friend, Dr. Nelson Glueck, and myself for the raising of a fifteen million dollar Development Fund to cope with the increasing responsibilities of this magnificently burgeoning movement—will be as naught unless we can find our way to some person-to-person dialogue with our God.

And in this search our Union must not be found wanting. For this Union is no mere service agency. It is that—but it must be much more. Together with our spiritual leaders in the Central Conference of American Rabbis, now headed by my distinguished classmate, Dr. Bernard Bamberger, we must lead the way in rediscovering the synagogue as a *Bes Ha-Mikdosh*, as a place of worship, of reverence and awe and aspiration. Short cuts and gadgetries, high-pressured "hard sell" campaigns or more subtle "soft sell" entertainment and atttractions, will not suffice. Penetrating, intrepid, must be our seeking. When the prophet dared to stand in the midst of an ardent throng pilgriming to their holy shrine on one of their sacred festivals, and to proclaim in God's name, "I hate, I loathe your feasts, and I take no delight in your solemn assemblies," he was ruthlessly attacking the most sacrosanct rituals of his contemporaries. We must be similarly radical.

We must ascertain whether we are not deluding ourselves with our superficial alterations in our prayer book which, despite its many sublime and surging passages, despite all the admittedly scholarly revision, of revisions of revisions, still repeats a number of archaic and anthropomorphic expressions of a long-outmoded past. "Reform

Judaism," as Rabbi Robert Kahn points out in the current issue of the *CCAR Journal*, "never did quite really *reform* the prayer book. For the most part it merely reduced it." Thus, we still pray to be "hidden in the covert of God's wings." He still "heals the sick"—though thousands of devout souls are wracked by the agonizing pangs of cancer; He still "loosest the bound"—though the stench of Auschwitz still stinks in our nostrils, though I read in the newspaper each day I was in Japan of men, women, and children who, like the contemporary J.B., still stagger blinded and with flesh rotted by the blast of Hiroshima. Yet are we enjoined to "enthrone Him as our *King*"; He still "givest them food in due season" though millions of His children starve.

Increasingly I have come to the conclusion that public prayers cannot be exclusively evaluated by us alone who read them from the *bimo*. Somehow, in the years when I was in my own pulpit and read our prayers week after week, I felt fairly satisfied, for my eyes were too steadily focused on my prayer book to be sufficiently perceptive of the "audience reaction"—the congregational response, or rather, lack of response. As one who more frequently of late sits in a pulpit chair or in the pew and who is thus able to watch not a few "slumped in unfocused torpor," mind-wandering or peacefully aslumber, I have become less content with the state of our *Union Prayerbook*. I have become more aware of the average layman's growing dissatisfaction but—"who listens?" Has he who may be filled with unsated spiritual hunger been called into consultation to help articulate the spiritual longings of twentieth century man? Really to reform our prayer book would mean, as Rabbi Kahn concludes, to "clear the ground and to start all over again with a master plan in which the salvaged riches of tradition would be cleansed, reshaped, planed, sanded, mitred, and fitted into an organic whole, a structure of worship which would be less like a museum and more like a sanctuary. Its architects must be rabbis, its builders laymen, musicians, poets, and playwrights."

Far more searching and candid questions must be asked concerning our forsaken houses of worship. We must inquire with our forebears, "Wherewith shall I come before Thee?" In fact, we must even more daringly ask, "Who is this 'Thee' whom we approach in this day?" Nor can we go it alone; neither rabbis nor laymen, nor Union nor Conference. We must more humbly reach out to those profound thinkers, creative spirits, sensitive poets and gifted composers of our time that together we may be able to find for the individual in the lonely secrecy of his own heart, as well as for the congregation in its exalted togetherness, some heavenly manna which may slake the thirst and appease the hunger which afflicts the whole of mankind today; the "hunger not for bread and the thirst not for water, but for hearing the word of God."

I.   I therefore urge that the Department of Worship be commended upon its basic research project which has now been launched with the cooperation of distinguished theologians and social scientists; and I recommend that, together with the CCAR, we strive to accelerate and intensify creative experimentation with synagogue ritual, music and liturgy so that we may enhance the reverence, beauty and spiritual richness of our Reform religious services and deepen the sense of the awesome presence of God among us.

But in Judaism, as we all know, faith and worship do not suffice. Knowledge, too, is required. Ours is no "Billy Graham" revivalism, no ten-easy-lesson road to "salvation." The buzzing drone of the Cheder and the pedagogy by rote of the erstwhile Yeshivoth may be outmoded, but the concept of *Talmud Torah K'neged Kulom*—of "Torah Study preceding all else"—is not. "An ignorant man cannot be pious," our sages audaciously suggested, automatically eliminating as ill prepared for Jewish leadership many members of our Boards, local, regional, and national. Dare we, in this Union, boldly take the lead in demanding first and foremost as a sine qua non for Jewish *religious* leadership at least some irreducible minimum of Jewish knowledge? Dare we require the possession not merely of financial resources but some certification signifying the acquisition of the rudiments of instruction in our exalted teachings so that our leaders may know—Jewishly at least—whereof they speak?

And we must continue to give support to those rabbis and lay leaders who are struggling so valiantly to establish higher standards in their respective congregations: The raising of the age of Confirmation, of the prerequisites for Bar Mitzvah, the acquisition of, at the very least, a passing acquaintance with our sacred tongue; we must strengthen them in their protest against the "infantilization" of our congregational life by the complete abdication of adult education:

II.   I therefore recommend that this Assembly commend the launching, with full-time staff, of our Department of Adult Education, and pledge the Union of American Hebrew Congregations to the unceasing effort to raise the level of Jewish literacy and Jewish knowledge among our adult congregants; and, conscious that synagogue leadership imposes upon the Jewish layman the profound moral obligation to equip himself with Jewish knowledge, I further urge that this Assembly recommend that our Department of Adult Education consider the development of curricular studies on Judaism which shall be regarded as indispensable prerequisites for lay leadership in all of our Reform synagogues, in our UAHC regional councils and federations, as well as on the Board of Trustees of the Union of American Hebrew Congregations.

From even the most superficial study of Torah we learn that such knowledge, like worship itself, is likewise not enough to discharge our responsibility as Jews, especially as Jewish leaders such as are here assembled. Of Judaism, more than of any other faith, it must be said that "a religion that ends with the individual, ends"; even with a worshipful, knowledgeable, individual Jew. Even so majestic an injunction as "walk humbly with thy God," which we have inscribed in imposing stone upon the facade of our Union House of Living Judaism (now in the process of even greater expansion as three more stories are presently being added), is preceded not merely in the specific words that follow but in the whole of Jewish tradition, by the mandate to "do justly and love mercy." And neither the Prophets nor the Rabbis spoke merely in glittering generalities. They did not need to be admonished—as one hypersensitive parishioner warned his preacher, "You may magnify and glorify and edify, but don't you dare to specify." They did not avoid explicit moral demands. And, like the Bible, does not the Talmud insist that one of but three challenges each man must answer to inherit *Ho-olom habo*—"The world to come," is whether he has been ethical in his business dealings? *Lo Hamidrash, eloh Hamaaseh*—"not even study," so exacting a compulsion in Judaism, is paramount—"but the deed." Yea, "the Lord of hosts is exalted through *justice*; the Holy One is sanctified through *righteousness*."

Let us, therefore, search and try our ways as children of this sadly and sorely fragmentized twentieth century society, afflicted with the agonizing "divisions of race from race, nation from nation, brother from brother," and return unto God whose paramount command has ever been not merely to "love the Lord thy God with all thy heart and all thy soul and all thy might," but, as that second noble sentence which we have inscribed on our Union House of Living Judaism has it, and which Buber has so intriguingly translated as, "Thou shalt love thy neighbor, he is like you."

This is Judaism; and with this as our standard, our course of conduct in the face of the New Frontiers thrown up by contemporary society becomes clear and commanding. No apter description of these frontiers of social challenge could be found than in the somber word which even the gentle Hosea was constrained to address to his wicked contemporaries, words which are as a burning fire within me, which strive as I would to withstand them, I cannot despite the tempting desire to provide some more delectable fare for this vast gathering, to play the presently popular game of "let's pretend." Let's pretend there are no bothersome problems of war or peace, of bombs and missiles and satelites, of bigotry, of a United Nations in a disunited world; to distil sweet pastor oil, to dispense numbing tranquilizers, to dispel your fears, and to "make you feel real good," as someone recently defined the paramount function of religion. No such snare to put you in a good mood for all the material demands which we must make upon you in the days immediately ahead; 10 per cent proportional dues and capital appeals— dare silence the truth—the stark, naked, inescapable truth contained in Hosea's timeless but most timely lament:

Hear the word of the Lord, O children of Israel,

For the Lord has a grievance against the people of the land.

There is no fidelity, no mercy, no knowledge of God in the earth.

False swearing and lying, murder, stealing and adultery.

In their lawlessness, bloodshed follows bloodshed—

Therefore the land mourns and all that dwell in it languishes.

"Therefore the land mourns and everything that dwells in it languishes." Could today's headline more aptly describe this hour which, ironically enough, it remained for Chairman Khrushchev to bring home to our time more vividly than almost anyone else when, in his recent message to the United Nations, he declared, "If all the means of destruction which mankind has possessed throughout his entire past were put together, they would constitute only an insignificant fraction of what the two or three great powers who have nuclear arms have at their disposal today? The explosion of one—only one, mark you, big hydrogen bomb would release a greater amount of energy than all the explosions set off by all the countries in all the wars known in the whole history of mankind."

And because so much inflammable material may be ignited by a single spark, by some ridiculous accident, or by the mental aberration of some stray pilot—because of this hideous prospect, it was this leader of the so-called godless Soviets who suggested the scrapping of every vestige of such world-convulsing dynamite. And the response? All manner of viewing-with-alarm and cautious reservations comprised virtually the only reply of the so-called God-fearing peoples of the world.

Now, I am not so naive—or "square," as the slang of the sophomores has it, as to be unable to "dig" the duplicity of a regime which holds in bondage myriads of its peoples, including some millions of our own brethren; which marched with murderous madness against the Hungarian masses yearning to be free. Far from condoning, I do join in vigorously condemning all the treachery of these tyrannical totalitarians. And yet—someone, some day, has to take this dare; has to call this bluff—if we are so omniscient as to *be certain* it is a bluff; someone has to take that giant step—bold and risky though it be—which will remove this specter of the searing of our planet in mutual mass incineration. Need we Jews be reminded that long centuries before Khrushchev, Isaiah had similarly urged the "beating of swords into plowshares and spears into pruning hooks"?

In the light of this appeal of our prophetic past, far more than out of confidence in contemporary Comrade Khrushchev, I plead and pray, in this context too, that we "search and try our ways"—that we examine scrupulously our possible motives for so unequivocally resisting even the concept of complete and total disarmament. Is it *only* our suspicions of the sly and satanic Soviet—well warranted as such distrust admittedly is? Or is there at least a modicum of fear not merely of their chicanery, but of the possible collapse of our economy, so largely geared to war; of the further nose-dive in the stock market already catapulted from its recent dizzy heights by the mere whisper of peace? Are we certain that our too spontaneous resistance is not prompted by a scintilla of dread that, once relieved of its own heavy burden of armaments, the Soviets—sans the need for huge personal dividends and individual profits—might indeed beat us in the economic competition which Mr. Khrushchev held so tauntingly before us?

I would plead with my fellow Jews, especially with those who are here assembled, whose forebears have had such spiritual valor as to face the most tyrannical of foes and yet dared to believe that they would survive his most wanton destruction; whose contemporaries have in every land been the first and foremost victim of war's depredations; who have come down the centuries, despite every provocation to battle and conflict, dauntlessly chanting *Ohev sholom v'rodef sholom*, "Loving peace and pursuing peace," to take a more sincere and serious look at this new frontier of a world which, as someone has concisely and truly phrased it, has become "too dangerous for anything but truth, too small for anything but brotherhood."

And, surely, my friends, if we have come here in the name of the Lord; if we stand in the presence of Him whom we call the Father of us all; if we would be true to each Sabbath's supplication to become "messengers of peace to the peoples of the world," then we must here and now rectify the failure of our last Biennial—contrary to the action of virtually every other religious convocation—to state unequivocally our opposition to a resumption of nuclear testing.

Though in some official sources the precise degree of fallout from Strontium 90 and Carbon 14 and Iodine 131 has been minimized, too much evidence points to the contrary; points to the irrefutable fact that, even if not a single additional bomb should be exploded, there is even now no way to wash the sky of those noxious wastes which will fall—not like the "gentle rain from heaven"—but as a death-dealing pestilence unto the third and fourth generations of the yet unborn. Who are we, especially we who profess to be believers in the fellowship of all humankind, thus to doom even a single fellow being to wander across the face of the barren earth, "their faces and hands burnt and swollen, with great sheets of skin peeled away from their tissues to hang down like rags on a scarecrow"? Who gave us the right thus to play God with helpless human beings as pawns; to pray not for "clean hands and a pure heart," but to pray and to probe for a so-called clean bomb, so clean that for days and weeks and months and years—perhaps even for centuries—the fallout from our nuclear tests may seep into the grains of wheat and drops of milk, polluting and poisoning all that which God hath bestowed upon us "for the blessing of all and the hurt of none"? Surely, our protest should split the sky against this ghastly business of the murder of the innocents.

The searching of our own souls and our return unto the Lord—as Creator and Protector of all mankind, to the God not only of Abraham, of Isaac and of Jacob, nor even solely of Israel, but unto the *Adonoy echod*, the "One God of all"—must inevitably lead us still further in our mission to be a "light unto *all* nations." Is any of us so jingoistic that we pray in our synagogues—or our neighbors in their churches—to the God of the United States of America only? Or to the God of the ever-so-self-righteous Western nations who have attained to some of their smug complacency through the plunder and pillage of "lesser breeds without the law"? The international anarchy of our time must indeed end—not merely through summit conferences which adjudicate this or that specific conflict—though we may well be grateful for this slight thaw in the disturbing and destructive cold war, but there must come a new insight into the Sovereignty of God rather than of men or nations, no matter how powerful nor with what supreme national ego they cast their vetoes.

We must therefore seek the strengthening of the United Nations, not merely by reforms in its machinery or techniques, but by the inclusion of *all* nations; we must seek to end this anomaly of including in its roster not a few dictator-ridden lands while excluding but one that comprises one-fifth of the human race.

III.   I urge this Assembly, accordingly, to speak out on these great issues of war and peace; to express, out of the depths of our prophetic Jewish tradition and social conscience, our unequivocal opposition to a resumption of nuclear testing; our appeal for the most serious consideration of a comprehensive plan for complete and total disarmament, and our utmost effort toward establishment of an all-inclusive United Nations. I likewise call upon this Union to join with all other religious groups in rallying the massive spiritual resources of mankind in pursuit of enduring peace based upon justice for all.

How true, likewise, Hosea's lament as we turn now to our domestic scene. Where lies the prime responsibility for all this "lying, murder, stealing, and adultery" which plague so much of our land? I fear that we must all confess our complicity, our silence which lends seeming assent to the hideous deterioration of the moral fabric of our cherished nation wherein men in high places and low mock at ethical standards and do lie and cheat and steal, in great things and small; on income tax returns and at the customs barrier as well as at congressional hearings and amid the councils of nations; wherein big business bribes legislators, labor leaders consort with racketeers; wherein commercial concerns rig TV quiz shows and indulge in phony doubletalk to promote their products, which Walter Lippmann recently and rightly dubbed the prostitution of merchandising; wherein rich rewards are reaped from rat-infested slums, kickbacks are taken for granted in ever-increasing areas; wherein even rabbis sometimes place themselves on the auction block to be sold to the highest congregational bidder; wherein adultery abounds in fact as well as in fiction and murder stalks the streets and countryside in juvenile rumbles and far-from-adult lynchings. There are many factors contributing to this breakdown in the moral fiber of our nation; but primary among them is the dumping of religious values—especially among the pampered and petted circles of our youth, even of our Jewish youth, as Rabbi Albert Gordon so accusingly points out in his penetrating *Jews in Suburbia*.

Might not our Torah be still the most formidable antidote to such a collapse of moral values? Did it not provide a "fence" against such pagan deterioration for countless generations of those who clung tenaciously to it? Did it not guide in ways not only of pleasantness but of decency those to whom wise and solicitous parents diligently taught it? May not the recapturing of such moral discipline as our Torah imparts ignite the spark that will kindle the fire requisite to burn out these nauseous impurities of our day?

This moral revolution must begin in the home, to be sure. But it must be supplemented by a more intense youth program in the synagogue, locally and nationally. How many juvenile delinquents emerge from our youth groups, our NFTY camps and conclaves? On the contrary, have we not witnessed the thrilling parade of these young boys and girls into the leadership of our congregational youth groups, the choosing of the rabbinate by increasing numbers of our NFTY alumni as their sacred calling? Do we not then contribute to the possible increase in this too general moral degradation by our failure adequately to provide facilities for larger numbers of our young people?

It is not alone for them, but for the very survival of our American way of life in which men will once again walk in security and decency, that:

IV.   I plead with this General Assembly to place high on its agenda a far more comprehensive program for the religious and moral training of our youth in synagogue, youth groups, institutes, conclaves, in private camps as well, and on the campuses of colleges and universities which, with all its resources and fine record of achievement, the Hillel Foundation cannot singlehandedly fulfill.

And now, to the most burning domestic issue of all. I must admit that I was sorely tempted to eschew, in this particular message, the New Frontier in race relations. For two reasons was I so tempted. In the first place, no one could be more aware than I that there has been no recent message that I have delivered at Biennials and Board meetings that has not included this theme and no one is more sensitive than I to the fact that there must be some who have consequently, no doubt, grown bored by such endless repetition. And, in the second place, surely I am not so obtuse that I am unaware of the specific spot in which we meet. But, as I am certain some of you suspect, neither of these considerations has prompted me to resist the temptation. Regarding the first—how can anyone desist from striking at any evil, time and time again, until that evil has been completely routed? And, surely, while none can fail to discern some little progress in this realm, it must still be admitted, as the prophet averred with regard to Israel—"they have healed but slightly the hurt of My people"; thus slightly, none can deny, has the hurt of the Negroes—also God's children—been healed.

And with regard to the second desideratum, which whispered to my sense of propriety, of *derech eretz* to avoid this theme because of our convening for the first time in this center so contiguous to the deep South, I could not evade the stinging reminder that the sin of segregation—as *sin* it is—is the monopoly of no region, for brotherhood is indeed indivisible. How provincial can some of us get? What I have in mind, as I plunge once more into this heinous transgression of God's Fatherhood and man's all-inclusive brotherhood, is the whole vast miasma of venomous racial hatred and segregation which rises like a stink in God's nostrils. As I wandered from city to city and country to country on my recent trip I saw but a handful of pallid white countenances amid the teeming millions of colored peoples who swarm the greater portion of this good earth's surface, I came face-to-face as well with the inheritors of cultures and moral disciplines which certainly compare favorably with our plethora of pistol-packing TV Westerns, our raucous rock and roll, our foul and filthy so-called "comic" books, our pornographic pulp periodicals, our stupid exhibition of "Can Can," as about the best some of us thought to offer to our recent Soviet visitor as the symbol of our vaunted Occidental culture.

And so, when I speak of the problem of race, I have in mind the savagery of white against black in South Africa, the humiliating allocation, gratuitously granted by all our white nations put together of a single seat on the Security Council of the United Nations to all the billions of colored peoples—and that one, incidentally and ironically enough, to Nationalist China; I have in mind the shameful Jim Crowism practiced by not a few labor unions on both sides of the Mason-Dixon line and the vigilantly guarded, lily-white neighborhoods of the North as well as the still sullen and stubborn resistance to the law of the land in too many parts of the South. Was it not Hosea who, likewise, warned, "In their lawlessness, bloodshed follows bloodshed"—and how literally was this prophecy echoed by that valiant-spirited Mayor of Atlanta after the bombing of our temple there, when he charged that "Every rabble-rousing politician is the godfather of the cross burners and the dynamiters." But it is not the rabble-rousing politicians alone who are the godfathers of this "bloodshed that follows bloodshed." If we take account of our sins of omission, who among us can plead "not guilty" to the lawless violations of the edict to "love the stranger even as the homeborn"? Most of us, by our moral passivity, have thus contrived to make "bloodshed follow bloodshed" and the day of judgment which will end the four-hundred-year dominance of the white race may come with a vengeance as these multitudes of the colored peoples of the earth may lose patience at long last with both God and white men and, in a wrath they have not yet known, they may rise to wreak their vengeance upon the infinitesimal minority which we pale-faces are doomed to become in the imminent population explosion which will see that population—principally colored—trebled in the next forty years.

But it is not out of fear for that dread day which, without repentance and restitution on our part, must come, but in a fervent plea to begin to translate the sublime teaching of our Jewish faith into the practice of our daily life that:

V.   I recommend that every Reform synagogue in our Union establish a Community Affairs or Social Action Committee to study and put into practice in each community the moral imperatives of our faith with respect to equality of opportunity for all peoples in every facet of daily life.

And in this fateful struggle all of us play our part for good or ill. For the issue, as Harry Golden puts it, is to be found in the anomaly which allows the Negro to supervise the affairs of our households, prepare our meals, make our beds, nurse our children—then place a million obstacles in his path when he wants to vote in an election while, at the same time, we shout for free and full elections behind the Iron Curtain; the issue is to be found in the paradox which grants the Negro wearing a white coat unrestricted access to the bedrooms and bathrooms and kitchens of our best hotels, and bars a Negro scientist from sleeping in their beds. The issue is to be discerned in the disparity of seven Negro women dying in childbirth to every one among us whites; of tuberculosis still ranking second as a cause of death among the colored peoples of our land and only eighth among us who comprise the white majority of Americans. The issue is to play the paternal, patronizing role of providing bail when a favorite Negro is in trouble, hastily to go overboard now to build schools for Negroes surpassing even those for whites—to give the Negro everything except recognition as a man; everything—except humanity. The issue is to have used and abused the Negress for decades as a concubine, and then to deny decency and equity to her and her offspring with the jibe, "Would you have your sister marry a Negro?"—forgetting that "what the Negro wants is to be our brother, not our brother-in-law"; that what he definitely does not want is the hypocritical double standard whereby the white man's licentiousness and license account for the scientific findings of anthropologist Melville Herskovitz that only 22 per cent of the American Negroes are undiluted by white blood, or sociologist Robert Stuckert's conclusion that 21 per cent or more than 28 million so-called white Americans are the offspring of such backyard dalliances. How many of us who petition Khrushchev to grant dignity and decency to our fellow Jews behind the Iron Curtain, who are invariably so quick to protest every deprivation suffered by our fellow Jews, have uttered a single peep of condemnation when hundreds of Negro homes and houses of God were brutally bombed? How many of us who seek the status symbol of the "right neighborhood" for ourselves ever take a positive step toward helping a Negro acquire human status by assisting him to purchase property on the street where we live? How many of us have blazed a trail to engage a Negro in our factory, office or shop not merely in the usual menial categories reserved "for Negroes only" but in any and every capacity to which he—even as you and I, who spend millions of dollars to end quotas and *numerus clausus* job exclusions for Jews—is equally entitled on the basis of merit alone? How many of us—I, as well as you—can count as friend, can say that we have treated as an equal in our homes, a single, solitary soul among the billions of colored folk on whom we profess God has likewise stamped His divine image? To all of us comes the challenging word of that superb Negro spirit, honored by some fifty universities, called the Gandhi, even the Jesus, of this generation, whose voice— whatever be the reasons, good or bad or morally neutral—is not to be heard in this Assembly. Since Martin Luther King was not permitted to bring to us here his gospel of soul force, of refraining from meeting hate with hate, I would be the unworthy mouthpiece of his searching charge which I fear applies to all of us—to me as well as to you: "It may well be that the greatest tragedy of our day is not the glaring noisiness of the so-called bad people, but the appalling silence of the so-called good people. It may be that our generation may have to repent not only for the vitriolic words and diabolic acts of the children of darkness, but also for the crippling fears and tragic apathy of the children of light. While the good people stood silently and complacently by," he adds, indicting too many among us, "the misguided ones acted. If every church and synagogue had developed an action program, had worked out plans to implement their righteous resolutions, Federal troops might not have been forced to walk the corridors of Central High School in Little Rock." Maybe the time has come for us Jews to learn from the Negroes who have learned so much from us, whose "spirituals" are so saturated with our Jewish faith, the kind of faith which has met violence with non-violence, hate with love, fear with valor, which impelled that old Granny, during the bus boycott in Montgomery, to decline the "lift" offered her as she trudged her weary way home after a back-breaking day of toil, with the words, "My feets are tired but my soul's at rest; I'se awalkin' not for myself, but for my children and my grandchildren."

"But wherefore should we Jews be in the forefront of this struggle?" the "statesmen," the oh-so-practical public relations oriented, civic-defense-minded among us inquire. "Let the Christian majority take the lead," let them abandon the blasphemous state of affairs which, despite occasional manifestos and courageous deeds on the part of Christian ministers (as of many rabbis) finds but a fraction of the churches of Christendom integrated, and which prompted one of its own savants, Dean Liston Pope of the Yale Divinity School, candidly to assert, "Some future Gibbon may well write that the church proved the greatest bulwark of segregated power in this generation; that the hour of eleven o'clock each Sunday morning, when Christians gather in their churches and sing paeans unto their Saviour, is the most segregated hour in the week." To be sure, Christians *ought* to be in the van. But since when did Jews take their cue from Christians, or from anyone else, rather than from God? Since the era of "peace at any price" began, no doubt! Strange irony, is it not? In times of the most brutal tyranny the Jew never looked to others for dissent from evil, but obeyed the behest of his God whatsoever the consequences. Yet, in this land of freedom we tremblingly seek the protective coloration of the majority. Judaism has ever warned us *not* to "follow the multitude to do evil." Therefore, though we must make every effort to join with our brethren of good will everywhere; though it would be more salubrious to our well-being, physical as well as economic, to lag behind; this is not the mandate of our faith. Can we not, like the similarly vulnerable Quakers, form cadres of freedom fighters to invade sacrosanct neighborhoods, inviolate employment agencies, bigoted PTA's, and give battle for new understanding, fair opportunity and common decency on the part of the white toward the black?

But in all these pressing issues it is not only as individuals or as separate congregations that we must thus rise to our high-born part, but as an organization likewise. Not merely in Biennial pronouncements either, but in day-in-and-day-out activity in our nation's capital where the destiny not merely of one nation but of the world is being largely determined. We have long anticipated and dreamed of a center of social action there in the heart of the free world where the life—and death—struggle between peace and war, justice and tyranny, brotherhood and bigotry, requires desperately the conscience, the conviction, and the concerted action of our prophetic Reform Jewish faith. Here we are not called upon to lead, to "stick our necks out," as it were. The voice of every other religious movement, save our own, *is* heard in Washington. I have been chided more than once concerning our conspicuous silence, therefore it is with consummate joy that I am privileged to announce that due to the magnanimous gift on the part of Mr. and Mrs. Kivie Kaplan of Temple Israel of Boston for the specific purpose of establishing such a center, we need procrastinate no longer. With gratitude to these far-visioned donors let us proceed forthwith.

But here, too, we must practice what we preach; we must obey the behest: "Physician, heal thyself"; to heed the logic of Isaac Mayer Wise who admonished, "Before Israel can discharge its high and holy mission to unite mankind, it must be united as one man." Most inglorious was the recent scramble on the part of certain Jewish organizations for the dubious distinction of waiting on Comrade Khrushchev. I do not say that given a greater degree of unity that august audience would have been granted. But I do say that the competition for honor and glory as to "who sits at the head table" of which the recent shameful competition to see the Soviet Chairman was but a single example; I do say that this ceaseless race to the President's ear in Washington and to the headline writers in New York, is unworthy of our ancient people. To quiver and quake before the specter of Jewish unity, to view with alarm the appearance of an "enclave," an "Elder of Zion conspiracy," is to believe the anti-Semite's fabrications; is to belie the whole of Jewish unity and the irrefutable testimony of contemporary Jewries elsewhere who do not tremble before such shibboleths and shadows. I have referred many times before to the welding of an all-inclusive Jewish community during my ministry in Canada—without any of the catastrophic consequences here concocted. I refer again to the anomaly, the irony of the Jews all through the ages fearing not to join brother to brother under the most ruthless tyrants and the most authoritarian regimes, and our apparent terror thus to close ranks under the permissive atmosphere of America.

VI.   I urge our Union, true to its pristine purpose in this direction, to continue in ever-more active support of the Presidents' Conference—a first tentative step toward some semblance of unity in American Jewry. A step, however, which must be pursued further, through such coordinating agencies as the Synagogue Council of America and the National Community Relations Advisory Council; pursued not hesitantly and from crisis to crisis but steadily and steadfastly, to the end that we may together rear a more mature, more continuously and consistently unified American Jewish community.

And there is yet another preface to peace in which we, as descendants of the prophets, must play our dominant role. I have mentioned before in other contexts, but cannot refrain from repeating now that which has been the most haunting and ineradicable memory of my world-wide trek of a little over a year ago. I have spoken of that single, most soul-shattering experience of hunger which afflicts more than half of our fellow beings throughout the world; the kind of hunger which finds men and women—and children, too—scavenging among the putrid garbage heaps of back alleys for a crust, nay, for a few crumbs of bread, for a scrap of rotting refuse, to keep themselves and their loved ones from premature death upon the sidewalks and pavements on which they live—or rather, barely exist—and die like flies. How, then, can we, who call ourselves a religious body, remain silent and inactive in the presence of some 237,000 storage bins in America bulging to capacity with spoiling surplus grain? With this present wheat surplus—to say nothing of the superfluity of other products—at well over a billion bushels, we could produce sixty billion loaves of bread or twenty-five loaves for every man, woman, and child on the whole far-flung planet! And yet, there are those who subsist on a lentil or two a day, and die because they are denied even this.

Nor can we blame our legislators for this paradoxical state of affairs. How easy, in our complex society, to absolve ourselves of blame by "passing the buck" to others and lamenting "What can little I do?" But how embarrassed and humiliated I was when recently the members of the House Foreign Affairs Committee chided and challenged me with the stinging query as to why so many of the "good people" of our synagogues and churches placed the lowering of the tax rate above their professed divine demand to "feed the hungry." Thus do you and I become the guilty ones; you and I, indirectly though it seems, become the murderers of starving children; your hands and mine become stained with blood. I plead that Jews and Jewesses of this Biennial Assembly, believing that the "earth is the Lord's and the fulness thereof," shall individually protest against this greed for gain and grain and that—each one of us—even at the cost of still more staggering and skyrocketing taxes, even perchance at the price of presently inconceivable deprivation on our own part, shall take more generous leadership not merely in providing for our own—as we so nobly and abundantly do—but all our fellow beings as well, and thus do our bit to rectify this blasphemy of God.

But some of you will recall that I found, throughout my travels, not alone this tormenting physical hunger, but a spiritual one as well. I found this not only among my co-religionists in the many lands in which they dwell, but among so many others whose ancestral faiths are seemingly inadequate for the complex and compelling new frontiers of our time. This same conclusion has impelled some of us to urge that we take literally the holy mission of Israel which bade Abraham to "be a blessing," not merely to his own kinsmen whose land and people he was bidden, as a matter of fact, to forsake, but to "be a blessing" unto all his fellow beings. Thus, there is much validity to the recently revived discussion concerning our erstwhile missinary enterprise, and I say erstwhile advisedly, for did not the New Testament describe our Hebrew ancestors as "scouring land and sea in search of a single convert"?

It is not to turn men of firm faith from their respective beliefs that such a renascence of Jewish missionary effort is urged by some among us, although I must confess that our Judaism does have much to offer to some whose religions steep them in a defeatism and despair at the very time when Israel's undying, yea-saying, life-loving message is so direly needed; whose guilt-ridden tensions require the uplifting faith to be gained not alone on the psychiatrist's couch but in the "courts of the Lord," where our triumphant pageantry of the centuries affirms, "God is"; life is not a "tale told by an idiot, signifying nothing"; men can—and yet will—make themselves and the world better.

It is, however, to such as are hopelessly adrift upon the sea of doubt and disillusionment and spiritual despair; to those who have no moral rudder to chart them through the troubled, tempestuous waters of our time, such as constrained the commander of the Japanese fleet, for example, during my visit to Japan, to call upon Christian and Jewish chaplains to assist him in formulating a program of ethical instruction for the men in his command; it is to these that we would proclaim in the words of our prophetic past, "Ho, every one that thirsteth, come ye and drink"; to offer to such as are thus ahunger and athirst a knowledge of that faith which has sustained our forebears through centuries of torture and turmoil. It was Leo Baeck who thus urged, "Our religion should approach humanity. We should not miss the time. Humanity, it seems, waits for us. Dare one say, Almighty God expects us?"

But this work must not be left to fly-by-night ad hoc committees and self-seeking opportunists who would somewhat too avidly seek converts by denegating their present faiths, as appears to be gravely possible in the vacuum which does exist in many places of the earth. It deserves the most serious consideration by this august body and so:

VII.   I urgently recommend that we explore, in our regional conferences as well as at our next Biennial, this timely subject of proselytizing and that, in the meantime, we pursue our deliberations in this realm with our spiritual leaders in the Central Conference of American Rabbis.

But before we presume to fare forth to the far reaches of the earth to convert the non-Jew, we had better consider first things first. For even if some of the fantastic rumors were true that millions await conversion to Judaism—a grossly and unforgivably irresponsible bit of misinformation—our table of priorities dare not be determined upon such a quantitative basis alone. Fewer in number, but just as spiritually hungry and athirst were the handful of my Jewish brethren whom I found in Hong Kong, in New Zealand, in Burma, in India, who likewise languish for the word of the living God and the way of a living faith. I stress the words *living* God and *living* faith. For virtually as pitiful and poignant as the demise of an individual is the tragic spectacle of the death of a once thriving, flourishing congregation and community. And so my heart did indeed bleed within me when I was shown lovely synagogues once pulsating with the chants of the chazan and the sweet sound of children singing praises unto the Lord, now silent as the tomb, utterly forsaken and forlorn. Forlorn, forsaken, dead because of the complete unawareness of that living Judaism which, with more vision, more imagination, more men, more means, we might bring to them. How heartrending the piteous plea which many of us heard at the recent conclave of the World Union for Progressive Judaism, for rabbis, for teachers, which welled up from these far corners of the earth. That is why our Board of Trustees is appropriating considerably larger sums to help discharge this inescapable responsibility which is ours to make of our Progressive Judaism something more than a restricted American sect, to make certain rather that it does become a world-wide movement. That is why we will soon welcome to this dynamic base of Liberal Judaism, where this contemporary expression of our ancient faith has flowered and flourished best, the headquarters of the World Union and why we pray for the full-hearted support by all our congregations of its first American President, Rabbi Solomon B. Freehof. That is why we have urged before and we urge again that in official resolution, and swift action, we shall seek, through cooperation with the College-Institute and the Central Conference, to find ways to meet these world needs.

VIII.   I recommend that this General Assembly wholeheartedly reaffirm our fealty to the World Union for Progressive Judaism and express our joyful welcome as the World Union comes to these shores and to its new quarters in the Union House of Living Judaism.

But money alone will not suffice. We need men as well. Surely, we need not be so liberal as to dare not to exact any scintilla of sacrifice—if sacrifice such service in distant places be—of men accepting the sacred calling of the rabbinate. We do not ask lifelong exile in some forsaken wilderness, as the youthful priest I met in primitive Nepal freely accepts for the remainder of his days. But we have some right to considerations of service as well as salary. That is why we urge the speedy implementation of the internship plan which would make just as imperative this service to our faith, whithersoever such service would take our young rabbis, as service to the flag now makes compulsory in the ranks of the chaplaincy.

IX.   I recommend that we express our unflagging support of a program which will provide the pecuniary means and the requisite disciplines to enable newly-ordained Reform rabbis and other trained personnel to serve at home and overseas our brethren who would otherwise be denied the message of our living faith.

That is why a large portion of our soon-to-be-launched Development Fund will be devoted not merely to structures of steel and stone, imperative though these be, on the several campuses of the Hebrew Union College-Jewish Institute of Religion, at our Union House of Living Judaism in New York, and similar centers of Reform Judaism in our key cities, as well as in our many youth camps, present and future; that is why, however, a large portion of these desperately needed funds will be set aside for mobile units, correspondence courses, synagogue and rabbinic subsidies, building loans and other tangible aids to help appease the spiritual hunger and slake the religious thirst of so many of our co-religionists who, both abroad and at home, require our indispensable assistance in money and in men.

X.   I recommend that this general Assembly pledge its support, both in resolution and in tangible response, to the long-delayed and urgently needed Development Fund for American Reform Judaism which is being initiated at this Biennial.

This Development Fund will enable us to proceed with the inescapable expansion of our Institutions in order to keep pace with the unprecedented growth of Reform Judaism, and to move into the new frontiers which challenge us. In addition to the physical structures needed by the Union and the College-Institute, the Development Fund is necessary to provide circuit-riding rabbis and mobile synagogues to rural areas, subsidies for rabbinical services, and new temples among our less privileged co-religionists, and in many other ways to bring the message of Reform Judaism to those who now languish spiritually and Jewishly.

Israel, too, is hungering for this message though, in these days and years of its desperate do-or-die struggle for existence, it may know it not. Though certain Israeli leaders and their avatars in our midst continue to predict the liquidation of our Jewish life in the so-called lands of our "exile" and consequently beckon us to forsake our homeland and our father's house to take up residence in that land which alone, so they aver, in defiance of the whole testimony of our Jewish past, vouchsafes the survival of the Jew and Judaism, we would continue to insist that we in this, to them, so Jewishly sterile land can match them: school for school, study circle for study circle, and surely, synagogue for synagogue. Much as we love the land of our religion's birth, we insist that deep are our roots in this soil. We must, of course, continue to rally to Israel's aid with our largesse, with our demands upon our own government to seek justice for this, our sister democracy, but we shall continue likewise to obey God's behest, spoken through the words of Jeremiah, to build *here* our houses, to plant *here* our vineyards, and to seek the peace of the land whither He has brought us. And here we shall continue tomorrow, as today and yesterday, to disprove the sneering disparagement of our labors by proving that a rich cultural and religious life can and does and will persist in flourishing in America, and the Kaddish which some have recited over our creative effort is premature—to say the least.

And, as for our contribution to Israel, if our cash and our bonds, our engineers and our scientists, our mechanical and technical know-how are so much in demand there, wherefore the seeming ban on our Reform faith? Dynamos and tractors "made in America" apparently are "kosher" and welcome; rabbis made in Cincinnati and New York are "trefe" and spurned. This is both a disdainful and false emphasis on the alleged exclusive materialism of America as well as a reflection on the equally mundane stress in Erets Yisroel. Both are egregiously in error. American Jewry has far more than gold to give and Israel has need of much besides money and scientific know-how. Was it not so passionate a *Hovev Zion*, a "lover of Zion," as Maurice Samuel who warned in *Level Sunlight*, "The greatest danger to Israel lies not in the possibility of Arab invasion or economic collapse, but in the loss of its character as being Jewish rather than merely Israeli"? Did he not suggest that, like chemical elements, the familiar utterance, *Mitzion tetze Torah*, "Out of Zion shall come the law," is reversible and might—must—read today, "*Into* Zion shall come the Torah and the word of God *into* Jerusalem"? Into Jerusalem—even from America, for world Jewry, Samuel concludes, "has something to teach even to Israel, and American Jewry is world Jewry's continental center. Israel cannot be rebuilt through a repudiation of America. Let world Jewry understand this—in Israel and everywhere else."

In the thronging cities of Jerusalem, of Tel Aviv, of Haifa, in the colonies and in the collectives, I have personally heard the appeal of not a few spiritually restless souls who have petitioned us for our moral and religious as well as our material aid. Fearlessly—for when has Reform not been attacked when it has pioneered in any land; dauntlessly—for wherefore should the Orthodox of Israel be more sacrosanct and untouchable than they were in Germany a century or more ago, in South Africa two decades ago, in Australia yesterday, and in New Zealand even now; dauntlessly and fearlessly, not furtively nor apologetically, we must lend hand and heart to those of our brethren in Israel who, precisely as those in India, in France, in Holland, in South America, are dissatisfied with Orthodoxy and do not yet know of the life-giving waters of our Reform faith. Without this life-giving faith I assure you, and I would like to assure Mr. Ben-Gurion as well, there is more danger of Judaism perishing in his land than in ours. We must overcome that timidity which permits millions garnered from Reform Jewish pockets to be spent exclusively on Orthodox Yeshivoth and "shuls" imported from the European ghettos and no more endemic to Israel than is our American Reform, while not one cent is allocated to such worthy academic institutions as the Leo Baeck School in Haifa. Therefore:

XI.   I call upon this Assembly, and others in our own ranks who have led in Zion's restoration, to protest the allocation of funds and facilities generously supplied by all segments of our American Jewish community, to but one religious group in Israel. Such facilities must be made equally and equitably available to *all* Jewish religious bodies within Israel.

Could spiritual cowardice go any further than the shameful silence of many of our Reform Jewish leaders in Zion's restoration in the face of this brazen wrong?

But how presumptuous to approach others in distant lands without practicing what we preach. How can we be an *or lagoyim*, a "light to the gentiles," in Japan, in Asia or to our own brethren in Zion, to the unsynagogued in South America, among the millions still unaffiliated even here in the United States, unless that light shines luminous and clear in our own lives, in all of our congregations?

We must first know ourselves that which we would proclaim to others. Ergo, the still pressing need for some manner of "guide to the perplexed" of our own Reform Jewry. Let none dismiss this widespread need by setting up the straw man of some kind of creeping sacerdotalism in which we would trade the role of the prophet for the robe of the priest and jettison our pursuit of righteousness in a plethora of rites frozen into an absolute and eternally coagulated code. Not one among us would prove traitor to our liberal faith by positing any such satirization—wittingly or otherwise—of what we earnestly seek. But surely there is need of some commitment other than the payment of annual dues (plus 10 per cent for the College-Institute and the Union, to be sure); some bare minimum of mitsvos, the acquisition of some rudiments of our tradition and teaching, and first and foremost, of some dedication to the demands of decency and dignity, of compassion and comradeship, of equity and justice, of love and peace toward all our fellow beings. This much of the "yoke of the Torah" is incumbent upon each one of us. Surely we have to provide some answer to the plaintive plea of myriads who write to me and others in the words of this letter: "What commitments are expected of me as a Reform Jew? What yardsticks apply? I don't know what is to be believed or followed. Lately I get the impression that every rabbi makes his own Sabbath as he sees it, as he wishes it."

To answer such fervent appeals, some of us would provide what Rabbi Rudin, in his presidential message to the CCAR last June, appropriately described as a "frame," so that "the way will be charted, not left any longer a maze in whose labyrinth we wander undirected and often out of touch with one another . . . . What ought we do to 'remember the Sabbath Day and to keep it holy'? What is possible and what is impossible? What must be done? What dare we not leave undone?" I trust it will be possible for us, in cooperation with the CCAR, no matter what false witness is borne against us concerning treason to Reform, to make a beginning concerning the "irreducible minimum" upon which Reform Judaism must build; to strive to ferret out the "point beyond which we cannot go except at our spiritual peril; to discover not how large shall be the house but only how small it dare be and still give all of its shelter."

Yes, there is spiritual hunger and thirst in our own land likewise. There are parched and sterile wildernesses here as well as abroad. My files are filled with poignant appeals for spiritual leaders, for teachers, for correspondence courses, for the breaking down of our disgusting and demeaning quota system in our youth camps; for the lowering of the high cost of joining a Reform congregation which is "pricing" vast numbers of eager, ardent Jews and Jewesses out of the synagogual market.

To rout all "ersatz" values which have crept into our once noble teaching of Torah requires vision, imagination, daring and selfless generosity on the part of those who, in their own congregations may well insist that religion, like charity, begins at home, but who must nevertheless learn that neither charity nor religion ends at one's doorstep, either of the home or of the temple. Swarming, affluent congregations, teeming with more members than they can possibly accommodate, even with the pell-mell rush of two and three "showings" on Rosh Ha-shono and Yom Kippur, must spearhead the attack on the vast multitudes of unaffiliated. They must become big sisters to those who sometimes separate themselves from the congregation, even the congregations of their fathers because of a spiritual hunger not appeased within their crowded and expensive gates.

But, above all else, we must practice what we preach in giving evidence that God does in truth count in our own lives and that Judaism is a moral imperative in our daily pursuits. Wherewith shall we come not merely before the Lord but before those whom we would win to our cause—whether it be some Japanese farmer in his rice paddy, disappointed and disillusioned with the erstwhile faith in his Emperor-God; be it to our brethren in a far-too-secularized state of Israel, or to those who unhappily are flowing from our fold into the beat and beatnik generation of our own land? Wherewith shall we appear before them in the market-place of ideas and ideals if not with clean hands and a pure heart? How shall we invite others to sojourn in God's tabernacle and dwell upon His holy mountain except as we, too, obey the Psalmist's behest to "walk uprightly and to work righteousness, to speak the truth in our hearts, to have no slander upon our tongue, and to do no evil to our fellow"?

To such a task would this high and holy convocation summon each one among us. It is a time for action, for dire and desperate action, as we face these new frontiers of an expanding universe, of enlarged human horizons. *Lech l'cho meartz'cho umimo-lad-t'cho*, we hear again the words of this Sabbath's Sidrah: "Go forth out of thy land and from thy father's house," go forth with all the pioneering zeal of our valiant fore-bears, that through thee and thy offspring all the peoples of the earth might be blessed." Get thee up, my cherished friends, my loyal and zealous co-workers, and march forth into the thick of the *milchomos Adonoy*, of the "battles of the Lord," mobi-lized against all the pagan idols of our time. *Avrohom Ho-Ivri*, Abraham was called "the Hebrew," our sages tell us, because *Kol Ho-olom Me-ever echod v'hu me-ever echod*, because "the whole world was on one side; he on the other." The world is on the side of faith in force; we must range ourselves on the side of force of faith; the world dispatches missiles to the moon and rockets into space; we must stalwartly send forth our spirit unto spirit and embark resolutely on our mission to mankind. It is a time, in truth, for what Leo Baeck called "the grand Jewish religion, the invincible Jewish faith . . . the great contradiction and reproach, the great proclamation and promise that once were a dynamic power, an historic vindication, a permanent problem to the world."

Lech l'cho, "Get thee up" out of the conformity and complacency of our "homoge-nized society" in which "the bland do indeed lead the bland"; get thee up out of that apathy which someone has aptly called the "fifth column of our time." Get thee up and become once more an *Am k'she oref*, "a people stiffnecked and stubborn for God, the Lord's most loyal opposition to evil." Get thee up, then, stand ye beside Abraham, smashing the graven images of his day, beside Moses, hearing God's ten great Commands, beside Jeremiah, Akiba, and all the myriads of our valiant forebears so that as faithful, faith-filled *Avde Adonoy*, "Servants of the divine," we may "hearken unto His voice," and obey His will. *Lech l'cho*—let us indeed leave our low-vaulted past, build us more stately mansions of the soul, rear us a temple of humanity, vaster—nobler than the last, till *all*, at length, are free, "leaving our outgrown shell by life's unresting sea." Let us catch the vision and challenge of one of America's most prophetic seers who so perceptively foretold the new frontiers we face today:

The earth, restive, confronts a new era

No one knows what will happen—such portents
    fill the days and nights;

Years prophetical; the space ahead is full of phantoms;

Unborn deeds, things soon to be— project their shapes around me;

This incredible rush and heat—this strange ecstatic
    fever of dreams, O Years!

Your dreams, O Years, how they penetrate through me!

(I know not whether I sleep or wake.)

The performed America—and Europe—grow dim,
    retiring in the shadow behind me,

The unperformed, more gigantic than ever, advance,
    advance, advance upon me.